rewired

brandon cox

PASSIO.

Most CHARISMA HOUSE BOOK GROUP products are available at special quantity discounts for bulk purchase for sales promotions, premiums, fund-raising, and educational needs. For details, write Charisma House Book Group, 600 Rinehart Road, Lake Mary, Florida 32746, or telephone (407) 333-0600.

REWIRED by Brandon Cox
Published by Passio
Charisma Media/Charisma House Book Group
600 Rinehart Road
Lake Mary, Florida 32746
www.charismahouse.com

Unless otherwise noted, all Scripture quotations are from the Holy Bible, New Living Translation, copyright © 1996, 2004, 2007. Used by permission of Tyndale House Publishers, Inc., Wheaton, IL 60189. All rights reserved.

Scripture quotations marked AMP are from the Amplified Bible. Old Testament copyright © 1965, 1987 by the Zondervan Corporation. The Amplified New Testament copyright © 1954, 1958, 1987 by the Lockman Foundation. Used by permission.

Scripture quotations marked NIV are from the Holy Bible, New International Version. Copyright © 1973, 1978, 1984, International Bible Society. Used by permission.

Cover design by Marvin Eans and Bill Johnson
Design Director: Bill Johnson

Visit the author's website at brandonacox.com.

Library of Congress Control Number: 2013952033
International Standard Book Number: 978-1-62136-519-8
E-book ISBN: 978-1-62136-520-4

While the author has made every effort to provide accurate
telephone numbers and Internet addresses at the time of
publication, neither the publisher nor the author assumes
any responsibility for errors or for changes that occur after
publication.

First edition

14 15 16 17 18 — 987654321
Printed in the United States of America

To Angie,
the love of my life,
whom God has used
to rewire me in
all the right ways

III. The "How" of Social Media

S OCIAL MEDIA IS the next big communication wave. I know this to be true because Saddleback is currently experiencing exponential growth as a result of our determination to stay in front of and use every technology and innovation at our disposal to reach people for Jesus.

Years ago I wrote in the first chapter of *The Purpose Driven Church* about the importance of "surfing spiritual waves." We don't create the waves; God sends them. We merely catch them, and wise leaders are not only on the lookout for the next big wave, but they are also ready to catch that wave.

The social media revolution is definitely a tsunami wave that must be caught. Any leader who wishes to have an increased influence for the sake of the gospel in our present world must understand the vital role that social media plays in our surrounding culture. And any leader who fails to increase their effectiveness in this area is already on the backside of an important tool in our modern global environment.

In *Rewired* Brandon Cox motivates not only leaders to embrace the social media wave but also to harness it for its greatest power of all—the power to spread the gospel farther and faster than ever before. When Brandon served as one of our pastors at Saddleback, he taught our staff to lead innovatively using these key principles and how to apply new social technologies to effectively expand our ministry outreach. Now, as he plants a Saddleback daughter church in northwest Arkansas, he's seeing tremendous results from these principles as they are put into action.

As a leader, you can only influence those whom you can reach. If you're truly serious about making an impact for the kingdom with the gospel message, take a listen to what this young church leader has to say and join the wave to reach everyone for Jesus!

—Pastor Rick Warren
Founding pastor, Saddleback Church
The PEACE Plan

xii

O N A PERFECTLY normal day in January 2010 I
received an e-mail from David Chrzan, chief
of staff at Saddleback Church, with an invi-
tation to connect by phone. At the time I was the
pastor at a smaller, established church in northwest
Arkansas, filling a fairly traditional pastoral role in
a fairly traditional church, so David's e-mail caught
my attention. I wondered why in the world the chief
of staff at one of America's leading churches would
be contacting me. We talked by phone an hour later,
and David invited me to attend an upcoming leadership conference at Saddleback—expenses paid.
OK. Sure thing!

A few weeks later I flew to Orange County and
enjoyed the hospitality of Saddleback's sweet-spirited
volunteers. They shuttled me from my hotel to the
church campus along with the conference speakers.
On the opening morning of the conference I slid
into the van and took the seat right behind Andy
Stanley and Jeff Henderson. The casual conversation
in the van was a little surreal for a bewildered young
pastor from a small church in semi-rural Arkansas.
The playing field was leveled only slightly when
Saddleback's faithful security team wouldn't allow
any of us to enter the building without our conference lanyards. For some reason my explanation—
"These two guys are speakers, and I have no idea

why I'm here"—didn't smooth things over entirely, but David's smiling face finally popped out of the green room, and he ushered us on back.

Hanging out backstage, I kept meeting people whose books and blogs I'd read, and each would ask, "So, what do you do here at Saddleback?" To each I would respond, "I have no idea."

At lunch David invited me to join him in a special meeting with some people from the world of publishing. I took my seat in a room with editors from *Leadership Journal*, *Christianity Today*, *Outreach*, and other well-known Christian magazines for a discussion about the direction of social media as it relates to pastors and ministry leaders.

The conversation taking place in the room was a thrilling one for me to be involved in. I had spent a decade and a half of my life in pastoral ministry and had always had a big heart for pastors in need of help and encouragement. And within the few years leading up to this conversation, I had also taken a keen interest in the world of social media. David had noticed my work as editor of *Fuel Your Blogging*, a site that was well respected within its field and was part of a larger conglomerate of online magazines for creatives.

I had also signed up for Twitter early on, before celebrities joined the game, so I was actively involved in the online conversation about church communications, branding, and marketing.

David kept batting questions in my direction in that meeting, and I kept speaking up in response to them—about trends in church communications, about social media and the way the church is (or isn't) using it, about the benefits of online networking. I often disagreed with others in the room, and since I felt I had little to lose, I shared honestly about the ways in which I felt American evangelicalism was falling behind in terms of communicating the gospel and connecting leaders together.

One of the theories offered by a participant in the room evoked an emotion-filled response from me. He postulated that pastors tend to escape the real world of their church ministry into the fantasy world of social networks, where they can find fulfillment in less-than-authentic relationships. I protested, "I think you have it backward. Pastors often walk out of the time warp of church on Sunday, where everyone is wearing a mask, and engage the real world in real time on Facebook."

I'm not sure if anyone in that room agreed with me, but I still think I'm right. Social media isn't an escape from the real world. It *is* the real world, whether we are ready for it or not. I have conversations with church leaders all the time who feel that walking into their churches is a trip back in time and a journey into a Christian subculture that is removed from the mainstream culture in which most people live. Church often seems more like a time warp back a few decades while social media is all about what is happening all around us right now.

The next day David took me to lunch, and over a Chick-fil-A sandwich he asked me to consider joining the staff of Saddleback Church to help reshape the ministry of Pastors.com. He had been searching for someone who had feet in two worlds—the world of ministry and the world of social media. He'd been reading articles I'd been writing and tweeting about for many months and was familiar with the work I'd been doing in the area of design and communication, and we discussed some of that work in telephone conversations over the next several months.

My initial connection with David began on Twitter. Let me say that again: a connection that eventually turned my whole life upside down began on Twitter. David is a quiet observer of leadership, and I had never connected with David until I received the initial e-mail inviting me to visit Saddleback. An online social network was the launching point for a relationship that remains vital to my life to this day.

Is there real, connecting power in online social networking? Absolutely. My story and the stories of many others illustrate the potential of social media to be a powerful tool for connecting people and spreading the gospel in today's context.

Let me be clear about this: The gospel itself never changes. The content of the message of the gospel has never needed editing. And the principle means through which the gospel is spread has never changed either—person to person in the context of community. But the *context* in which we share the gospel and the *tools* we use to do so are changing constantly.

The book you hold in your hands is about how to share the unchanging truth of the gospel in a constantly and rapidly changing world—and why you should care about using new technological tools to do so. We'll explore other technological changes that happened in history and how they served as hinges for change in culture and morality, so as to provide a greater perspective on the impact of new technologies for the work of the gospel. We'll examine some of the vital principles for effectively connecting with our present culture. And we'll talk about some of the most popular tools and networks out there and how you can harness their potential for good.

My great hope for this book is that it motivates you to embrace change in a healthy way and that it motivates you to engage your world with a timeless, hope-saturated, life-changing message—that Jesus is still and always will be the answer to humanity's greatest questions.

Part I

WHERE DID SOCIAL MEDIA COME FROM?

Chapter 1

GOD INVENTED SOCIAL MEDIA

Y OU MAY HAVE picked this book up with a feeling of skepticism. I don't blame you. After all, social media is a fad that will soon pass, leaving behind plenty of ruined social media "experts" and snake oil salesmen who promised to have a monopoly on the cutting edge. The entrepreneurial start-ups that are highly overvalued in Silicon Valley will fail (again), the Internet-driven economic bubble will burst (again), and social media will die.

Right?

There is a sense in which social media *is* a fad. That is to say, the *term* is a fad. In fact, I sometimes grow weary of hearing it myself. I probably receive more spam than you do promising me the ability to get rich quick by jumping on the social media bandwagon early.

But beyond the hyped-up terms, is there something resilient about social media? I believe so. In fact, I would say social media is a concept much older than the human race itself.

Let me explain.

ALL MEDIA IS GOD'S MEDIA

The phrase "social media" is relatively new, but the concept is as old as the hills. The word *media* refers to information. That information might be words, sounds, or visual imagery. Just a decade ago we would brag about hosting a "multimedia" event, meaning an event that contained spoken words, visual images, videos, and sound. Before the dawn of the Internet, the invention of the printing press, or even the discovery of papyrus, information passed from one person to the next through conversation. Media has always existed in some form or another.

So media is simply information. We typically use the word *media* to refer to news and happenings or to data, such as a movie stored on a DVD or an album stored on a CD. But media is really a very broad term that refers to anything that can be talked about.

Then there's the fact that all media exists in the mind of God before anyone else. When scientists make a new discovery, the world considers it a breakthrough, but they're really just uncovering something God knew all along. When archaeologists dig up a long-gone civilization, it changes what we know about the past, but God was there and knew about it all along. There isn't anything God can learn, since God is the source of all media.

Adrian Rogers, the former president of the Southern Baptist Convention, used to ask, "Has it ever occurred to you that nothing ever occurs to God?" Several others have said something like, "If it's true it isn't new, and if it's new it isn't true." The point is, God knows it all. The Bible calls Him the Alpha and the Omega, the beginning and the end. We know God is outside the confines of time and therefore existed before the beginning and will always exist after the end.

But His identity as Alpha and Omega means even

more than this. "Alpha" and "omega" are the first and last letters of the Greek alphabet, the universal language of the world in the times of the New Testament. Anything that could be written was expressed using the twenty-four letters of that alphabet. The point is that God is the originator of and final authority on all things true. All media—at least all media that matters—is God's media first.

GOD'S NATURE IS TO BE SOCIAL

Now consider this: media has always been social, because the Creator of all things is social.

Of the four Gospel writers, John is the one who goes back the furthest in his account of Jesus. Mark begins with Jesus's baptism, and Matthew and Luke start with His birth and a detailed genealogy, but John takes us to a special place—the place where God, as Trinity, initiated everything we know to be real. He starts with Jesus as God in eternity, before the creation of the world and mankind:

> In the beginning the Word already existed. The Word was with God, and the Word was God. He existed in the beginning with God.
> —JOHN 1:1–2

I'm not sure if you understand the implications of this title given to Jesus, but being the "Word," or *logos* (the Greek term), signifies that Jesus is the expression of all that is in the mind of God. All truth, all knowledge, all that is real and eternal is shared in the person of Jesus Christ. If media refers to information, then God is the ultimate media producer. He is the author and revealer of truth, and all that can possibly be known in the universe originates in His divine initiative.

But there is a second significant principle John lays out for us, and that is that the Word (Jesus) was *with* God for eternity. He uses the word *with* twice, perhaps for emphasis. The Father and the Son have been together forever, and they will continue to be together forever. The idea of intimacy finds its roots in the relationship the three members of the Trinity—the Father, the Son, and the Holy Spirit—have always enjoyed and will forever enjoy with one another.

It is this unbroken, eternal relationship between Father and Son that made the cross so painful. The physical pain Jesus felt in His crucifixion must have been excruciating. But even greater was the pain He endured emotionally and socially as, for the first time in history, His social circle with the Trinity was broken. Jesus, who took on the weight and penalty of the sin of humanity, was forsaken by the Father in a punitive act of judgment against rebellion—*our* rebellion. The pain of broken fellowship for those few hours at the cross merely highlight an important truth about God: He defines intimacy.

Intimacy literally means "to be fully known." We might know people—our spouses, our parents, our friends—in a way we would describe as "intimate," but what we experience is merely partial intimacy. The Father's relationship with the Son, however, is truly and completely intimate.

To say that the personalities of the Trinity are "close" would be an understatement. They are, in fact, *one*. The oneness of the Trinity is so difficult to comprehend that our feeble minds can hardly begin to grasp it. We come up with trivial illustrations, such as the three parts of a single egg or the three forms water can take, but all our illustrations fall short. The fact is, God is social in a way we are simply not.

But we were created with the capacity to be social.

God Made You Social

Since God, by His nature, is infinitely social, it stands to reason that when He began His creative work, He made a race of people that would reflect His relational ability.

When God created Adam, the Bible says He "breathed the breath of life into the man's nostrils, and the man became a living person" (Gen. 2:7). When I was young, I would chuckle a little bit when I would read that verse as I reflected on the awkwardness of the moment. Imagine waking into existence for the very first time to be staring eye to eye in the face of your Creator, who had just finished breathing up your nose.

I now realize the awkwardness of that situation is the result of our tendency to draw back from such intimacy. In other words, it is because God was *so* close to Adam, invading what we would refer to as his "personal space," that makes the moment so deeply meaningful. God made Adam for a face-to-face relationship with Himself and for real companionship. In the same chapter God

5

declared, "It is not good for the man to be alone. I will make a helper who is just right for him" (v. 18). A social God recognized the need within His creature to be social with others. So He made Eve and paired them up so they might enjoy intimacy and relationship with one another.

But God has gone further than merely granting us a social nature and putting us on the same planet. He's even decided to gather us all into one great big happy family. The Bible says, "God decided in advance to adopt us into his own family by bringing us to himself through Jesus Christ. This is what he wanted to do, and it gave him great pleasure" (Eph. 1:5). God has a big family and values every single one of us on a social, relational level.

So think about it this way: the Garden of Eden was the very first social-networking arena, and the family God started creating that day was the very first social network. It was God's idea for information to be spread friend to friend. It was God who placed into mankind all of His creative ingenuity, and it is by putting our creativity to use that we reflect the image of our Creator.

Further, it is God who creates the capacity for technological advancement and scientific discovery. He has been fully aware of all of our gizmos and gadgets since before the foundation of the world. Social media didn't originate with the invention of e-mail or Facebook or Twitter. Social media is a concept known and shaped in the mind of God. In other words, God invented social media.

GOD ARRANGES THE TIMES FOR THE GOSPEL'S SAKE

If all we have said so far is true—that God is social, that He created you and me to be social, and that He created earth to be a social place—then it stands to reason that God's heart is to so arrange history that His grand purpose of reconciling people to Himself and to one another would be accomplished through the significant shifts and movements we've observed on this planet. In other words, if the grander story of God is the redemption and reconciliation of mankind to Himself and to one another, then what emerges throughout history is the evidence that God is setting the stage for this reconciliation all along the way. From the oral culture of the Stone and Bronze Ages to the poetic and artistic emphases of the Renaissance, God utilizes each new turn in the human story to lead us to the conclusion that He invites us to know Him.

Soon after Creation God performed the first wedding ceremony, binding Adam and Eve together in a "one flesh" union. He commanded them to know each other fully and intimately. And this institution called marriage became the first institution upon which society would be built. Marriage has a highly social agenda.

God called Abraham from the land of the Chaldeans to journey to Canaan with his family to establish his temporary home there. Hundreds of years later the Jews returned to that land and arrived a couple million strong. God divided them into tribes and clans and families and

7

households. He kept intact their social structure, which continued until the rise of the empires of the Babylonians, the Persians, the Greeks, and the Romans. Under their rule the Jewish people were exiled and returned, disassembled and reassembled. The Old Testament is a narrative of God continually and repeatedly restoring the fellowship of His people. For much of the Old Testament era the history of God's people and His activity among them was handed down from one generation to the next orally and conversationally.

Around the New Testament era God sovereignly guided the Jewish people to establish synagogues—local houses of worship where they would gather together. These synagogues held schools and became the focal points of their communities. And beyond the Jewish people, He arranged history for the building of the Roman roads, the expansion of the Greek language into all the Roman Empire, and the establishment of trade routes on land and sea. Why? To create pathways for the gospel and gathering places where the apostles would spend time preaching and presenting Christ to the world.

In other words, globalization is not exclusive to our modern era. It's been happening since the major empires of biblical times. In more recent centuries God used the Renaissance to enlighten the world through the technology of the printing press, and the first book to roll off of Gutenberg's world-changing invention was the Bible. It couldn't have happened at a more important time. In the age of Tyndale, Calvin, and Luther the mechanism for putting the Word of God into the hands of the average individual believer came at just the right time and certainly had plenty to do with the kickoff of the great Protestant Reformation.

A rapid succession of discoveries and inventions has shaped the last century and a half: electricity, the telegraph and telephone, radio and television, and the Internet. These innovations have fueled the Industrial Revolution, allowing mass production and distribution of all kinds of products, including Bibles and Christian books. Resources for churches have never been more plentiful.

No Time Like the Present to Get Social

God is the great designer who has masterminded a plan to put people in relationships with each other. "Viral" isn't a concept the inventors of YouTube conjured up—God has always determined to utilize the viral nature of human relationships. Ideas spread like diseases from one person and culture to the next, including the story of God. We talk about the effects of sin and the need to spread the good news of Jesus, but the fact is, even without the presence and effects of sin, the story of God and His glory is still worth sharing. It's the greatest idea in history. And the capacity for its dispersion is broader than ever. While the apostles utilized the Roman roads, we take advantage of the advent of the Internet age and the wonder of the social media revolution.

We who believe in Jesus Christ have the greatest story

imaginable within us. We were made to be social and to connect with other human beings in intimate relationships. And God has paved the way for the good news to spread like wildfire.

So it's time to get started. It's time to be social, for Jesus's sake.

The questions this book seeks to answer are rather simple: How do technology and culture influence one another? What are the current technological and cultural shifts taking place around us? And how will these shifts provide new and innovative ways to spread the gospel around the globe? God is certainly up to something...but isn't He always?

Reflection and Discussion

1. What do you think it means to say that "God invented social media"?

2. In what way is God social? What does it mean for God to be the author of all media? How does it change your outlook on current social-networking trends to know these things about God?

3. How do we see God orchestrating history in such a way that the gospel has been able to make a broad impact, from the time of Jesus throughout the life of the early church?

4. If God made you to be a social creature, then how are you doing? Do you see improvement and increased intimacy in relationships over time?

THE DAY THE CONVERSATION DIED

MANY PEOPLE SAY silence is golden, but Robert Frost reminds us "nothing gold can stay." Silence can be either a blessing or a curse. In a noisy world a bit of solitude goes a long way to calm our anxious souls. It creates the margins necessary for our sanity and offers us the capacity for meditation and focused thinking on that which is true, pure, and honest. Silence can be a really good thing.

But silence has a dark side too.

Silence is awkward. We humans don't care for it much. In fact, we avoid it at all costs as long as we're awake. We install stereos in our cars so we don't have to drive in silence. We plug headphones into our MP3 players so we don't have to go for a walk in silence. We keep our televisions on even when we're not watching them so as to avoid the possibility of the air remaining devoid of sound waves. One of the most uneasy moments we face is being in a social setting in which no one has anything to say at a given moment.

The fact that we do this isn't the fault of silence. It's rather our discomfort with it. We just don't like the awkwardness of it.

And there's a reason for that.

Sin's Deafening Silence

Why are we so uncomfortable with silence? I believe it has something to do with the beginning of the history of silence. In the previous chapter we began to grasp the concept that God is social and that God made mankind to be social, placing Adam and Eve into a garden meant to be a setting for continual conversation. And one fateful day in that garden the conversation died.

The tempter came to Eve and dangled before her the possibility of possessing God-like power, and she, being deceived, ate the fruit and gave some to her husband, who also ate. The next scene is tragic. The Bible describes it this way:

> When the cool evening breezes were blowing, the man and his wife heard the LORD God walking about in the garden. So they hid from the LORD God among the trees. Then the LORD God called to the man, "Where are you?"
> —Genesis 3:8–9

God is described in this passage as "walking about in the garden." The invisible God who is never confined to space or time wasn't literally walking around like a man. This is simply the Holy Spirit's way of communicating to us that God was present with Adam and Eve in the garden, seeking them and desiring conversation with them. But none was to be found because Adam and Eve were hiding in the shame they felt over their sin.

When I read this story, I think about how I love playing hide-and-seek with my kids. I've learned that the younger they are, the worse they are at playing the game. I play hide-and-seek to win. For me it's a match of wits to see who can find the most creative and unthinkable hiding place and then to remain there as quietly as possible, barely even breathing. But for my kids, especially as toddlers, it's not about hiding but about being found. Their excitement over the thrill of being found causes them to giggle and bubble over in anticipation, erupting into laughter when their eyes finally meet with their seeker. We more experienced adults know that hiding requires silence, even if the silence is awkward.

So Adam and Eve hid themselves in silence, withdrawing from the disapproving glare of a holy God. And in their self-protection they brought pain to the heart of their Creator, who so prizes the companionship of His creatures. For God, the death of the conversation was tragic.

W. A. Criswell tells this story about the moment the conversation died:

> A wise and experienced homiletics professor, teaching his class of young ministers the art of preaching, called upon each one to read this section of the Book of Genesis. As each student stood up to read the passage, the old professor was watchfully waiting. Some read it as though God were simply asking a question, "Adam, where art thou?" Some read it as though God

were angry. Some read it as though he were indifferent. But one young preacher read it in pathos, with a sob in his voice, "And the Lord God called unto Adam, and said unto him, Where art thou?"

The old professor looked at the youth searchingly and said, "Young man, you will be a great evangelist. God has given you a compassion for the souls of men. When God came into the garden in the cool of the day and called to the man He had made, God was broken-hearted as He asked where he was and what he had done."[1]

Because of the entrance of sin, our ability to relate to one another and carry on healthy conversations has been broken, and we see the shattered remains of broken relationships all around us. Divorce is familiar to half the homes in America. The orphanages of the world overflow. Nations battle other nations.

This mass division results from the brokenness of humanity. Families are falling apart, and the body of Christ continues to fragment because we can't get close enough and honest enough with others to fully know them and be fully known by them. Our lack of conversation has resulted in fear, which leads to hatred, which leads to racism, prejudice, and inequality in the world.

Individuals feel the weight of social isolation too. Suicide, in 2010, was the tenth leading cause of death in the United States, accounting for 38,364 deaths.[2] The issues behind this statistic are complex, but one of the glaringly obvious factors is the isolation and loneliness we feel in a society that is supposedly more connected than ever before. The effects of sin are undeniably destructive, and the death of our ability to build healthy relationships began the day Adam and Eve, in the midst of paradise itself, rejected the healthy relationship that existed between themselves and their Creator.

Embedded in the story of Adam and Eve's separation is the seed of our own story. All of human history has given evidence of the brokenness of our relational ability and the resulting hunger in our hearts for restored intimacy. The world has a need for redemption and for restoration. And the very moment that need arose, as the relationship between mankind and God was fractured, God went to work executing His perfectly prewritten plan of redemption and reconciliation.

SILENCE RUINS SO MUCH

The world is lost, and its only hope is the gospel. Therefore what it needs is the missionary voice of the church going to every people group on the planet with the story of Jesus. The silence that resulted from sin's curse is one of the church's chief enemies. Satan has little to do with keeping the world blinded to the gospel if we aren't sharing it. In fact, silence itself can be a sin of omission. While God is calling us to express our praise and our worship for all to hear and to speak the name of Jesus in every corner of the earth, our silence is direct disobedience to His command.

But the problem of silence is more complex than simply not sharing the gospel enough.

Silence preserves injustice.

There are places in the world where families and children suffer daily from hunger, malnutrition, persecution, and slavery. Their lack of resources presents a further problem: a lack of access to any kind of media or communication outlet. Until others speak out on their behalf, silence is their ever-harassing and persistent enemy, and it is therefore the enemy of the gospel. Consider the massive success of the Kony 2012 campaign that made a household name of an obscure tyrant and forced the world to notice the issue of kids enslaved as soldiers.[3]

Silence kills relationships.

Almost never does a married couple seek counseling at the moment one spouse is initially injured by the words or actions of the other. Instead, we bottle things up, build resentment, and blow up or melt down in a destructive downward spiral. But honesty and intimacy are far more difficult than silence, so we remain content not to speak of our hurts. When marriages and families are falling apart, you can bet silence has something to do with it.

This same brokenness resulting from silence affects every other kind of relationship. Parents and children become estranged from one another. Neighbors stop greeting one another. Tribes and nations go to battle because of the unspoken tension that silence creates.

And when we aren't talking about the emotional and

relational problems that exist in human relationships, we certainly aren't sharing the gospel with one another. The gospel is a conversation that is often awkward in and of itself. In this way, the gospel is hindered.

Silence solidifies shame.

Two kinds of sin feed off silence. The first is the sin we commit. If we keep silent, failing to confess our sins to God, the One who is faithful and just to forgive us and to cleanse us, then we get trapped in an unending sin cycle.

Then there are the sins others commit against us. Abuse, neglect, gossip, slander, and violence do great damage to us emotionally and spiritually—and while these sins are not ours to own, we carry shame over them nonetheless.

For instance, I once saw a piece of artwork drawn by a small child. It was dark and scary. He had chosen primarily black and red as he outlined the members of his family. My wife, Angie, who works with children in foster homes as a therapist, asked me if I had noticed the "X" drawn on the child's mouth. I had not. She explained it's something therapists spot because it's typical of children who have been told repeatedly not to tell anyone what has been done to them.

Shame keeps us silent, and the progress of the gospel is stopped. When we remain trapped in the shame of our own brokenness, we retreat from the comforting voice of the gospel, and we are left powerless to give or receive its message. As I mentioned previously, silence has its dark side.

Silence seals the destiny of people without Jesus.

I'm not a big fan of guilt-induced evangelism. It's fairly easy for pastors to tell sad stories and condemn an audience for its lack of compassion and concern, but I don't believe Christians are silent about their faith because they don't care about people. In fact, I believe most believers want to share their faith. Social media has even made witnessing a reality for many believers who have never shared their faith before. From YouTube videos of creative presentations of the gospel through graffiti and rap to electronically distributed copies of Christian classics, people can pass on a wealth of gospel-centered material easily. And more importantly, even a short status update can convey a powerful personal testimony of conversion, healing, or maturing spiritually.

But we do sometimes need a reminder about the devastating effects of our choice to be silent about the most important subject on earth. When I slip into a pattern of silence concerning evangelism, I often recall the words of Charles Spurgeon that are written in the front cover of my Bible:

> If sinners will be damned, at least let them leap to hell over our bodies. And if they perish, let them perish with our arms about their knees, imploring them to stay. If hell must be filled, at least let it be filled in the teeth of our exertions, and let not one go unwarned and unprayed for.[4]

It's Time to Speak Up

Silence has a tendency to ruin things—not everything, mind you. Remember what I said at the beginning of this chapter about its benefits. We often need to cultivate silence in our lives in intentional ways for the health of our minds, bodies, and spirits, especially in this day and age when so much clamors for our attention.

But we were made by our Creator to connect with others, and intimacy is a deep and abiding need of every human heart. We need to know and be known.

And so, it is time to speak. It is time to connect. It is time for us to emerge from our cocoons to engage the rest of the world in a silence-shattering conversation about eternal things. Silence fosters oppression, but you can speak up for those without a voice. Silence traps people in shame, but your voice can communicate grace to those trapped in sin. Silence endangers and threatens to destroy delicate relationships, but you can say the words needed for healing. It's time to speak.

Not only is it time to speak, but it's also time to get loud. I believe we have something of eternal value to share. The gospel is worthy of a hearing in the public square and the private coffee shop conversation. And here's the good news: it is altogether possible that our culture's renewed emphasis on social networking and personalization may help create the capacity to fight the problem of silence more effectively.

The good news of Jesus is life changing, and if new tools have been handed to us that provide the power to spread the message farther, then let us speak with enthusiasm. Jesus said it this way: "What I tell you now in the darkness, shout abroad when daybreak comes. What I whisper in your ear, shout from the housetops for all to hear!" (Matt. 10:27).

Let's break the silence!

Reflection and Discussion

1. How did sin in the Garden of Eden destroy God's concept of social interaction and relationships? How does sin continue to hinder the relational ability of human beings today?

2. What is the problem with silence? What problems in the world are allowed to exist when silence rules?

3. How can breaking the silence about global issues provide us with the capacity to see real change around us?

4. Are you currently involved in social networking? Are you speaking up in the arenas available to you? Without getting overloaded, are there areas of online social networking where you need to extend your voice and expand your influence?

Chapter 3

RELATIONSHIPS CAN SAVE EVERYTHING

I T WAS ROBERT Frost who wrote of a neighbor who said, "Good fences make good neighbors."[1] In other words, establishing distance and proper boundaries helps us get along better with other broken people—at least, so we think. Don't get me wrong—boundaries, in their proper place, can be a good thing. I'm not saying we should live like a sieve, letting anything and everything, including other people's destructive habits and abusive behaviors, into our lives because, hey, relationships are priority number one.

What I am saying, however, is that keeping people away usually makes us feel safe, and not in a good way. Think about it: Adam and Eve started a fence-building trend when they sinned against God. They barricaded themselves off from God. They hid from His presence, afraid of the pain of being intimately known in their newly discovered sinfulness. Their decision has had destructive relational ramifications ever since.

It took only one generation for humanity's relational dysfunction to manifest itself in the most extreme way—the complete devaluing of one human life (Abel's) by another (Cain), which culminated in the act of murder. When confronted with his crime, Cain's response was simply, "Am I my brother's keeper?" (Gen. 4:9, NIV). In other words,

"I'm my own man. I'm not responsible for others. I live my life as an isolated individual and not in relationship to my fellow man."

Cain's act of hatred was only the beginning.

In the American Revolutionary War, 4,435 patriots lost their lives on the battlefield. In the Civil War, the death toll was more than 360,000. And World War II witnessed over 400,000 deaths.[2] There have been, in our short national history, more than one hundred different wars and conflicts involving our military. But these numbers don't even begin to scratch the surface of what the planet has seen since the days of Cain and Abel. We are a people at war with one another, and the conflicts don't appear to be slowing down anytime soon, despite all our peacekeeping efforts.

War might seem to be the epitome of the relational division of humanity, but it is not the only piece of evidence. Consider the horror of the Holocaust, the vehemence of our political battles, the tragedy of racism, the tyranny of slavery, and our general propensity to protect the interests of ourselves at the expense of other people. We are immersed in a culture of broken homes, fatherlessness, motherlessness, and an epidemic of divorce. As I write this, I hear Rodney King's famous words echoing in my ears: "Why can't we all just get along?" Perhaps the best answer to King is, "Because we're broken, and because we're silent."

We're broken as individuals, and we're broken as a human family—and our solutions for the brokenness aren't working. The best humanity can offer as a fix for the brokenness is the issuing of new rules and new laws. We sign treaties, clarify boundaries, and create a criminal justice system that punishes those who act out their relational illnesses in ways that harm other people.

We also create rules and boundaries in our relationships with one another. Like the characters in Robert Frost's poem, we stack our rocks between one another in the hopes of keeping people at a safe distance—out of our pain, out of our hearts, and out of our lives. When we live on the basis of rules, we simply need to know what lines shouldn't be crossed. If we comply with one another well enough, we'll get along adequately. We'll never be close, but we'll survive on the planet together.

God's Plan for Fixing the Brokenness

God has a different idea about how to fix our biggest problems. While Adam and Eve were hiding, God was approaching, seeking, and searching. While humanity drew back from its Creator, He put on human flesh and invaded the world in the form of His Son, Jesus, to seek and save that which was lost. God is all about the business of reconciliation.

Paul said it this way:

> For God was in Christ, reconciling the world to himself, no longer counting people's sins against them. And he gave us this wonderful message of reconciliation.
>
> —2 Corinthians 5:19

27

The cross was certainly a place of punitive justice when the wrath of God against the sin of humanity was poured out upon Jesus. But the cross was also a place of redemption. On the basis of Jesus's death and resurrection we can have a restored relationship with God and find avenues toward healthier relationships with one another.

God's plan to heal the breach between humanity and Himself involves bringing people under the influence of the gospel so that they might come to know Him. Knowing Jesus personally is everything. Beginning a relationship with God through His Son is the one and only way to have eternal life, to understand His plans and purposes, and to make an everlasting impact on the world for God.

The apostle Paul spoke of how much he valued his restored relationship with Christ when he wrote to the Philippians:

> Yes, everything else is worthless when compared with the infinite value of knowing Christ Jesus my Lord. For his sake I have discarded everything else, counting it all as garbage, so that I could gain Christ and become one with him.
> —Philippians 3:8–9

It is in knowing a person that we come to understand them and therefore have peace and intimacy with them. As I have said before, the word *intimacy* literally means "to be fully known."

God has not only offered Jesus to reconcile the world

to Himself. He has also assigned the further work of reconciliation to His people. In other words, He asks the reconciled to go and reconcile others. From one relationship to the next, God desires to bring the world together again. In our present age God is miraculously making this happen through the institution of the local church.

How the Church Can Save the World

Bill Hybels has well said, "The local church is the hope of the world."[3] But at first glance, it would seem that Hybels is off base. After all, the church is seriously flawed. From the seven churches of Asia Minor mentioned in Revelation 2–3 to the evangelical landscape in modern America, the church is guilty of legalism, traditionalism, materialism, apathy, immorality, and pockets of heresy. We've hurt and maimed believers and have done a seemingly inadequate job of fulfilling the mission of God in this world.

How in the world can an organization with so many faults and failures possibly be the answer to the world's greatest problems? It's because the church, with all of its flaws, occupies a special place in the plan of God for the ages. Jesus died for the church and is miraculously cleansing it over time by washing it with His truth. God has always been gathering a family to Himself, and in our age He is accomplishing this gathering work through the church. He empowers the church for the commission that He Himself has issued to "go into all the world and preach the Good News to everyone" (Mark 16:15).

The New Testament gives us quite a few metaphors for understanding the nature of the church. The church is described as a fellowship, a family, and a flock, all of which show a picture of a church that gathers people together into a covenant community. That community is most often talked about in the New Testament as a local, visible assembly of called-out people. Because it's local, visible, and made up of brothers and sisters in a spiritual family, the church is the ideal mechanism for fostering relationships that draw people into a relationship with Jesus and one another.

If relationships can save everything and the church is the ultimate relational community, then it stands to reason that the local church, with all of its flaws, is the one great hope to draw each new generation into the ever-expanding family of God.

THE CHURCH THAT GETS IT GETS RELATIONAL

Some churches *get it,* and some churches don't. Those churches that get it can be found in many denominations, in many cultural settings, and in many shapes and sizes. Some are denominationally governed, some are democratic in nature, and others are led by elders or boards of directors. Some have beautiful cathedrals with stained glass while others meet in coffee shops, living rooms, and movie theaters.

The churches that are the primary hope of this

generation are quite diverse, but they do possess some common characteristics.

First, churches that communicate the gospel effectively in this current culture first possess a biblical theology of eternity. To be timely with our message, we need to start with timeless truth and never-changing theology. A church's compassion for a lost world is usually found to be in proportion to its understanding of heaven, hell, and the absolutely crucial nature of evangelism, as well as its deep-rooted conviction that the gospel can change the face of any community and the entire world in this present age.

In addition to a biblical theology, churches that offer real hope understand that relating to the surrounding culture is of utmost importance. No, it isn't about accommodating sin. And it isn't about imitating secular practices to make the gospel more palatable. It's about understanding the heart language of the culture in which we find ourselves missionaries.

One of the common fears among Christians is that if we don't stay on the cutting edge and familiarize ourselves with every new gadget or social platform that takes the Internet by storm, we'll get left behind. Our fear often leads us to discouragement and isolation. We think, "If we can't stay ahead of the curve, why try?" But reaching the culture has never been about leading the technology industry in any age. Instead, it's about being relational.

Churches That Don't Get It Won't Make It

Change and growth go hand in hand. But when I talk about change among Christians, I always hear the same replies:

- "Change for the sake of change isn't good."
- "Change might be inevitable, but we should take it slowly and carefully."
- "We shouldn't change if we're going to leave people behind."

I get this. I really do. I spent a dozen years pastoring churches in which I was too afraid of people to push for the change that would have been necessary to generate new life and momentum. I sometimes reserved voicing the need to press forward in adopting new ministry methodologies because of a consensus of people who defended their personal preferences in spite of the need for more effective evangelism. I often chose sparing feelings and being liked over breaking traditions dear to some.

But my life and leadership style changed dramatically when I joined the staff of Saddleback Church in Southern California. In Saddleback's atmosphere staff members often cut through the chaos to remind one another of the phrase "Hey, we're fast, fluid, and flexible." Ministries develop out of conversations in a matter of days, changes in ministry approaches are implemented on the spot, and projects and initiatives are sometimes killed off quickly when their ineffectiveness would hold the church back. The beauty of this mentality is the ability to respond to the Holy Spirit's leading instead of being stuck in institutional traditions.

I heard this phrase enough that it eventually became a core value for Grace Hills Church, which my wife, Angie, and I are planting with Saddleback's support and purpose-driven DNA. We worded the value like this:

> We stay fast, fluid, and flexible. There are no sacred cows. We embrace the pain of change for the win of seeing more people meeting Jesus.

So, to those common refrains against change, I say this: Change for the sake of change can be good if it forces us out of our comfort zones into reevaluation and revival mode. When we change too slowly, the culture around us moves on without us, leaving empty and outdated church buildings in its wake. And as for leaving people behind, God certainly doesn't approve of heartlessly leaving people behind, broken by disunity. But the mission of redeeming a lost culture for God's glory matters far more than pleasing people or providing a safe and comfortable home for the frozen chosen.

There are two rules for churches that find themselves unable to relate to a dying and decaying culture. First, don't mess with God's truth. Principles never change. And second, *do* mess with any system, structure, or strategy that becomes ineffective in carrying out the mission. If it's dead, bury it. If it's broken, fix it, scrap it, or replace it. If it's not growing, diagnose it. If it's comfortable, challenge it. If it's a strategy that looks like a middle-aged son still living in his mother's basement whose only job is playing video games, raise its rent and kick it to the curb when it no longer pays up.

Change—now! Move fast. Stay fluid. Remain flexible. And embrace the pain of change for the win of seeing more people meet Jesus.

HELP FOR THE RELATIONALLY DISADVANTAGED

God knew we would struggle with this relational thing, even inside the church, so He gave some rather helpful suggestions and guidelines that we often call the "one anothers" of the New Testament. These may or may not be familiar to you, but try to hear them with the ear of one who is engaging the culture via social media:

- "Be at peace with each other" (Mark 9:50, NIV).

- "Love one another" (John 13:34, NIV).

- "Be devoted to one another.... Honor one another" (Rom. 12:10, NIV).

- "Live in harmony with one another" (v. 16, NIV).

- "Accept one another" (Rom. 15:7, NIV).

- "Agree with one another" (1 Cor. 1:10, NIV).

- "Serve one another" (Gal. 5:13, NIV).

- "[Forgive] each other" (Eph. 4:32, NIV).

- "Submit to one another" (Eph. 5:21, NIV).

- "Encourage each other" (1 Thess. 5:11, NIV).

- "Spur one another on toward love and good deeds" (Heb. 10:24, NIV).

- "Pray for each other" (James 5:16, NIV).

This list is only partial, but it's a good starting checklist as we answer the question, *Am I being relational?* Part of the redemption story is the beautiful benefit of our being able to relate to one another within the body in a new way.

It's not easy. We will be misunderstood, and we will misunderstand. We will be hurt, and we will hurt. We will be criticized and rejected, and we will be guilty of the same at times. But if relating to each other wisely honors the nature of redemption and brings glory to God, let's go for it.

We live in the most connected yet disconnected age since the Garden of Eden. We are split seconds away from communicating with anyone on the planet, and there are more ways to meet more new people than ever before, but we are lonelier than ever, and our isolationist ways have left millions struggling through life without friends, without partners, and without a forever family.

Our assignment is to go and tell everyone about the love of the One who can help, can save, and can make everything different for all of eternity.

Will our message be heard? Perhaps. Keep reading, and we'll talk about the shift that must happen for the church to really connect.

Reflection and Discussion

1. How does the cross provide a way for our relationship with God to be restored? And what are the implications of our having a real relationship with God rather than simply coasting through life?

2. How does redemption affect our other relationships in lives? Our marriages? Our work relationships? Our relationships with our neighbors?

3. Why is it painful for churches to make the necessary shifts to become more relationally oriented rather than program oriented?

4. Would you describe your church as "relational"? Why is it so important for churches to be relational? How can your church be more relatable?

Chapter 4

M Y MATERNAL GRANDFATHER had a pretty amazing story. He grew up poor in rural southern Kentucky, and after finishing the eighth grade, he went to work like most of his friends. For much of his adult life he was a poor milk truck delivery driver who could barely make ends meet for his family. But about halfway through his life he had an idea for a business and launched Willoughby Communications, a company that salvaged used telecommunications equipment and resold it to companies who needed to update their equipment but couldn't afford the newest, hottest, fiber-optic systems on the market.

His idea worked. He wound up traveling to almost every state, doing business with small- to medium-size companies and eventually reached his lifelong dream of earning a million dollars. His ingenuity and entrepreneurial passion had paid off. I sometimes wonder if my own passion for planting a new church reflects a spirit of optimism and the drive to create something from nothing I inherited from him.

My grandfather's business was successful, but the reason it was successful probably tells us a lot about why the church struggles today. If my grandfather were dealing in church methodologies instead of telecommunications equipment, he could have made

NOW IS THE TIME TO GET REWIRED

quite a fortune among Western church leaders. Why? Because he made money helping companies update just enough to stay alive but not enough to compete in their rapidly changing markets. The companies with whom he did business knew they needed new wiring but usually weren't willing to risk going all the way to completely modernize.

Sound familiar?

We Have a Wiring Problem

In the world of church leadership we strive to push forward while waiting for all of our constituents to catch up. We're afraid of the unknown, so we avoid unfamiliar territory. We're afraid of staying where we are because we know that spells our eventual death. And we're afraid of disappointing people, so we take little risks and make little tweaks that don't really change the game.

We have a wiring problem in evangelicalism. We have the right message, but we're struggling to connect to the culture. For a couple of decades the church sought to change merely its external practices in the hopes of attracting the nonbelieving world. We updated our music styles, retranslated the Bible dozens of times, and offered a more come-as-you-are atmosphere in our weekend services.

But our real problem is deeper. It's our inner wiring.

We are wired for building institutions.

Learning from the business world has done wonders for the church. We produce more skilled leaders. We're organized for more structured growth. We manage money better and advertise and promote our events with greater clarity.

The downside is that we wind up protecting the organization and feeding the machine. Churches often find themselves too big to risk failure, too far along to change directions, and too institutional to get in the dirt with broken humanity. Obviously churches ought to do the very best they can to manage their growth and streamline their systems for effectiveness, but if we are no longer willing to take the risks we took years earlier because of potential failure, we need to rewire our thinking. What are we really protecting? And what's the opportunity cost of doing so?

We are wired for mass communication.

The advent of radio and television changed everything for the church. In fact, the church was an early adopter of mass broadcast technologies. Some of the longest-lasting radio and television programs in existence are broadcasts of church services.

But with the social media revolution has come a resulting shift to interpersonal conversation—rather than mass broadcast—as the primary vehicle for transferring ideas. The church struggles to rejoin the conversation happening now between individuals.

One of the struggles in this regard is that mass communication seems easier. Even though it costs much more than spreading a life-changing message socially, it's also far easier to sit in an office and send messages over the airwaves, via direct mail, or over the Internet without actually interacting with individual people. The more we can reach, the better, right? Perhaps, but failing to engage with individuals among the masses will spell the death of many churches.

We are wired for program-based ministry.

Someone invented the terrible idea that if we could just do more, meet more, and offer more, growth would be inevitable. So we have a ministry for everyone and everyone in a ministry. Even in churches of a few dozen faithful volunteers, we tend to exhaust people with the number of ministry programs we like to list in our brochures. There isn't anything wrong with specialized ministries, but there is danger in cluttering the pathway to spiritual maturity with distractions.

A relational church de-emphasizes programs and crazy, event-filled schedules and instead focuses on a process for growing people. In other words, they avoid giving the impression that in order to become spiritually mature, people need to attend three worship services, two Bible studies, a committee meeting, and a potluck each week. Instead, they gather on the weekend for corporate worship, scatter during the week in small groups of some kind, and spend the rest of their time living out the values of disciples serving the world for Jesus's sake and taking Jesus to a world desperately in need.

Groups and individuals doing life in this more relational, organic kind of culture seek to model biblical values and serve their communities without the approval of committees or the red tape of institutional hierarchies.

Small groups in a relational church context exist far more for the purpose of connecting people to the life of the larger church than for the dissemination of church traditions. In our church, for example, we encourage people to start small groups whenever and wherever they'd like, without seeking the approval of institutional leadership. When a group echoes our vision and values and remains accountable to pastoral leadership, we empower them without controlling them.

We are wired for protecting the status quo.

Our human nature craves to be liked, to have the approval of others, and to generally keep everyone happy. When personal preferences trump our missional mandate from Jesus, we fail to ask, "How can we reach our community?" Instead, we ask, "How can we reach our community and still make sure this is a comfortable place for our longtime faithful members?" History proves, however, that it's impossible to change the world and protect the status quo at the same time.

Companies that fail to adopt new technologies will be swallowed up by the competition, but they often must make significant organizational and personnel changes to make it happen, which causes friction and challenges the status quo. Across the land are hundreds of large church buildings or former church buildings where a congregation held onto tradition and accepted the status quo instead of embracing and adjusting to their communities in terms of culture and ethnicity.

But protecting the status quo is a death sentence.

We are wired for combating the culture.

There have always been moral issues to be addressed in society, but the church often creates an us-versus-them atmosphere about them, which kills the conversation that could take place about the gospel. Churches often fight political battles without caring for wounded people. We protest abortion without ministering to women at the crossroads of an unexpected pregnancy. We fight the gambling lobby but don't offer solutions for people who struggle with gambling addictions. Perhaps what we need is an us-*for*-them mentality that values all souls enough to listen to the viewpoints of others. Anytime the church declares war against the unchurched culture, everyone loses.

It's Time for an Upgrade

I'll never forget the first computer I ever owned. It was a Packard Bell, and when we bought it from Sears, it came with a whopping two megabytes of RAM. Of course, we would never need all that speed, but we didn't want to have to upgrade for a decade or two. And even though the hard drive was adequate, we knew we could store extra data on double-sided floppy disks, providing a computing capacity that would preserve us well into the next century. A year later we spent two hundred dollars to upgrade the RAM from two to four megabytes. In two more years it was scrap metal.

We've learned in the last decade or so to expect our equipment to be quickly obsolete. We know when we plunk down the cash for a new cell phone, the newer model will be available and cheaper in just a few months. It has been said that in the business world, whoever has the best technology wins. I'm not sure that's universally true, but it definitely has some merit.

In the world of church leadership and church communications we have a terrible tendency to lag behind in our adoption of technology. This hasn't always been the case, as we've already illustrated with the church's rapid adoption of radio and television mediums. But because of certain stigmas ("It's a youth thing," "It opens a Pandora's box of immorality," "It breeds narcissism"), we're a bit behind the curve. Obviously we don't need to jump into any cultural innovations blindly, but a healthy awareness and timely embrace of new communications capabilities are essential to effectively getting the gospel out in the present generation.

So how do we upgrade our evangelistic wiring?

We need to plug into God's power.

This might seem basic, but it's too often overlooked. In many pockets of evangelicalism we've settled for what we can produce in our own power. It is entirely possible to build a growing, successful organization with the right amount of money, talented leaders, and skill for marketing. This is not a wholesale indictment of churches that possess these qualities but rather a warning against trusting in these qualities apart from God's blessing. When we really value God's power, prayer becomes the priority over performance.

Don't make the mistake of forging ahead into a new method of carrying out the mission without seeking the blessing of the One who owns the mission. In fact, you might want to stop at the end of this section of the book and spend some time praying for God's clear direction as you seek to develop new ways of communicating the gospel.

We need to learn to speak human again.

In the year 2000, three years before Myspace existed and four years before Facebook entered the world, some amazingly insightful guys wrote *The Cluetrain Manifesto*. They saw the social web coming before it arrived. In the preamble to their ninety-five theses, they wrote these words to "the people of earth":

> A powerful global conversation has begun. Through the Internet, people are discovering and inventing new ways to share relevant knowledge with blinding speed. As a direct result, markets are getting smarter—and getting smarter faster than most companies.
>
> These markets are conversations. Their members communicate in language that is natural, open, honest, direct, funny, and often shocking. Whether by explaining or complaining, joking or serious, the human voice is unmistakably genuine.
>
> Most corporations, on the other hand, only know how to talk in the soothing, humorless

monotone of the mission statement, marketing brochure, and your-call-is-important-to-us busy signal....

But learning to speak in a human voice is not some trick, nor will corporations convince us they are human with lip service about "listening to customers." They will only sound human when they empower real human beings to speak on their behalf.[1]

Now, go back and read that again but replace the words *companies* and *corporations* with the word *churches*. It's a bit chilling. As long as we are determined to keep our churchy wiring, we will fail to connect with our culture. And as long as we keep our grip on our programmatic, ritualistic, institutionalized version of the church, we will fail to capture the hearts of the hurting desperately in need of relationship.

Jesus was wildly popular among the common people of Israel because He refused to keep the Pharisees happy by dressing the part of the religious leader. He became human, spoke human, hurt as a human, and touched humanity in every respect. We should do the same.

We need to lead proactively.

Reactive leadership is killing us. When Jesus declared the "powers of hell would not conquer" the church He built, I don't think He was kidding around. (See Matthew 16:18.) We have nothing to fear—the ultimate victory is already won. So why, then, do we hide in our bunkers waiting for the next cultural battle to come along? Why do we try to start saving our churches only when they are almost dead? And why do we attempt to understand technology and innovation only when it seems safe to do so?

It's time to go on offense. By "offense," I am not attempting to invoke a military image. I'm simply saying it's time for the church step up and lead, which requires tremendous courage. It means going first and being an example to others.

I get that this is hard. I really do. When I was a student at Western Kentucky University, I saw this play out in the speech communication classes I took. Every time we came to a spot in the curriculum that required class members to give a speech, the question from the professor would inevitably come: "Who would like to go first?" Then came the long pause, during which students shifted uncomfortably in their seats.

The one who goes first has to break the ice and make mistakes without the benefit of seeing others figure it out first. Going first is not our natural inclination, but in a world in need of restoration and in a constant state of cultural flux, it's really time. The alternative just isn't an option anymore. Faulty wiring restricts the flow of God's power through us. Even worse, bad wiring can be rather destructive to the church, spelling our eventual death if we don't assess and adapt our approach and our language to each new generation.

It's time to lead. It's time to do some rewiring.

Reflection and Discussion

1. Of the wiring problems mentioned in this chapter, which do you find your church or organization struggling with? Which do you struggle with personally?

2. Take a little time to attempt to diagnose any other wiring issues not already mentioned. How might you be trying to reach the current culture with out-of-date communication methods?

3. Look at some recent pieces of communication from your church or organization (sermon transcripts, bulletins, brochures, website copy, etc.); look at them as though you have no clue about your industry's jargon. Have you been speaking human?

4. Why do you think the church often stays behind the culture rather than stepping out in front to lead it? In past generations the church shaped the culture's art, music, architecture, and other mediums of communication. What has changed in our generation?

Chapter 5

EMBRACING OLD VALUES IN A NEW WORLD

H ISTORY REPEATS ITSELF. That's not just a cliché. It's true. To put it another way, human beings have a tendency to make the same dumb mistakes over and over as the story of earth unfolds. From eight-tracks to faulty systems of government, we tend to forget the shortsightedness of our earlier attempts and ignorantly press forward, trying concepts that have proven themselves utter failures in the past.

On the flipside, history has seen its revivals of good ideas and strong values. Or as J. Edwin Orr put it:

> There have been instances in the history of the Church when the telling and retelling of the wonderful works of God have been used to rekindle the expectations of the faithful intercessors and prepare the way for another Awakening.[1]

I believe the social media revolution has revived some old values the church tends to miss in its evaluation of the moral condition of our modern world. Yes, we're facing challenges to the moral fabric of humanity at an alarming and increasing rate, and the church is right to be concerned about this. But in the middle of cultural decay there is arising a renewed emphasis on values that originated in the heart of our Creator. We have the unique opportunity right now to harness the embrace of those values for the greater proliferation of the gospel message.

The Values of the New Social Culture

Technology drives cultural change (papyrus, the printing press, mass media, etc.), and we also understand there's a cyclical nature to this change. That is, while technology drives cultural change, our cultural values often determine the kinds of new technologies we demand and design. For example, Apple has a reputation for making things simpler. Steve Jobs was obsessive about reducing the number of features, functions, and buttons on devices to give every product a clear, singular focus and a simple interface for the user. I don't think it's any accident that Apple's biggest successes came with the move toward *simple*. I also don't think it's merely coincidental that within the same cultural generation, there has been an increasing demand for churches to be less complicated and program driven and driven more by purpose and simplicity.

Consider how the invention of the telephone suddenly made people. This technological innovation changed our culture by allowing people to communicate quickly and personally in spite of geographical distance. And in turn, as we adjusted to quicker communication, we then demand that new technologies reflect our new culture value. We demanded texting because of how the telephone had changed our cultural values and now we expect our texts to be answered as rapidly as a phone call.

Papyrus changed our culture from an oral one to a written one, and in turn we demanded more scrolls of knowledge. The printing press made written material accessible to common people, and in turn common people demanded more and better books. The television exposed us to cultural values from far-off places, and in turn we've demanded that technology's entertainment value be incrementally better with every new television released so that we can consume more.

With the rise of online social media, some values are surfacing that perhaps haven't been as important to the church or to the secular world as they have needed to be. Facebook, Twitter, and other platforms are causing us to reconnect with otherwise "lost" friendships and to meet new people we never would have met without these tools. And in turn the cultural values created by these platforms become part of our wiring and cause us to demand tools that flesh out those values in an improved way. Myspace introduced to our culture the value of discovering new and old relationships online. In turn we demanded better than Myspace, which is now a virtual ghost town. We've turned to Twitter and Facebook, which are further shaping our values so that we will demand new and better tools soon.

What are the cultural values created in a social media-saturated culture?

Authenticity

Nothing goes unnoticed anymore, especially inauthenticity. The word *integrity* comes from the Latin word *integer*, which refers to a whole number, not a fraction. All integers are multiples of one whole number. To live with integrity means to live as one whole person, then—the same in public as in private.

Now, it's true we have an innate fear of discovery. Most of us are afraid of being truly and fully known by others because we're aware of our faults, our mistakes, and our negative tendencies. But we live in a world that is changing quickly in this regard. We share more about our lives than ever before—through status updates on Facebook or by posting photos of random daily moments on Instagram. Granted, sometimes we share far too much information with far too little substance, but we're more OK with being known than ever.

What's more, we care about the authenticity of others perhaps more than we ever have in history. When a leader fails morally, when a celebrity blows their stack, when a company does something stupid to profit off the pain of others, we know it. And we know it quickly. The world of social media demands integrity from us as never before, and this is a good thing.

Authenticity isn't a new idea, though. It originated in the heart of God. Jesus displayed it as He walked with an openness never before seen by the culture into which He stepped. He invited the disciples to travel with Him, to sleep wherever He slept, to eat with Him, and to get to know Him fully and intimately. He never once put up a front or wore a mask. You always see the real Jesus when you read about Him in the gospels. He was, is, and always will be truly authentic. It's a good value for us to relearn today.

What's more, this is one of those values the church needs to recover within its ranks. We could stand to learn a bit about authenticity from the world of social media. There's a reason our surrounding culture doesn't appreciate our condescending tone toward people with values different from ours when we've failed to live out our own values well. There's a reason people don't respond when we assume a different personality in the pulpit, pronounce God's name with three syllables in that "preacher voice," and dress to impress instead of being ourselves. The church that hides in its cathedral under a cloak of churchy-ness will fail to reach the current generation. We need to be rewired for greater authenticity than ever before.

Others-centeredness

Social media has created the capacity for a whole new slew of scams. There are plenty of people who utilize systems designed for authenticity in inauthentic ways—hence, the large number of fake accounts designed to lure prospective spenders into black holes of so-called marketing opportunities. But as time goes on, people have wised up, and the majority of social networking users help police the online culture well. Consider the increasingly prevalent usage of the phrase "add value." It's a core idea of social media that basically says the way to build a stronger relationship with friends, customers, and even strangers is to create content and facilitate connections that benefit them, expecting nothing in return. The idea of "adding value" is why so many companies offer free white papers or e-books about their area of expertise with no strings attached. They are "adding value" so as to facilitate a relationship, knowing that their constituents will return when they have expanded needs.

There are still plenty of people in the world of social media who make the mistake of connecting with others via a conversation that starts with, "Hey, look at me! Look what I have to offer! Read my blog! Click my links! Buy my stuff!" Thankfully, people are starting to wise up to a much better way of beginning a friendship. It's far more important to start with, "Hey, tell me about you! What do you offer? What can I learn from you? How can I help you?"

By way of example, not long ago we moved Rick Warren's Ministry Toolbox e-mail newsletter to a new e-mail platform that allowed us to get to know our subscribers a little better. Now we send a personal e-mail to every new subscriber that asks three questions:

- Where do you serve?
- What are you passionate about?
- How can we at Pastors.com serve you?

As a result, I've heard stories from leaders all over the world, and we've been able to respond to their stories by creating content that more effectively serves them. Sometimes we even get the chance to respond with a specific resource a leader needs in a moment of crisis.

Now, who invented the concept of others-centeredness? God did. Jesus lived it out on earth as God in the flesh, and we are urged to emulate this characteristic of God. As Paul said:

> Do nothing out of selfish ambition or vain conceit, but in humility consider others better than yourselves. Each of you should look not only to your own interests, but also to the interests of the others. Your attitude should be the same as that of Christ Jesus.
>
> —PHILIPPIANS 2:3–5, NIV

God is, scripturally speaking, God-centered. He is the supreme and central figure in the story of redemption. But the way in which He has chosen to derive glory for Himself is to act in completely others-centered ways. God has repeatedly invaded human history, visiting earth in the form of angel-like messengers to Abraham, Paul, and others. He provided Himself a Lamb in the form of His Son, Jesus, who clothed Himself in human skin and served others, fed others, healed others, taught others, and eventually gave His life as a ransom for others. And God is preparing an eternal home, a new heaven and a new earth, so that He can offer to others an eternity in His joy-filled presence.

Generosity

In our social media age we're making up new words—such as *crowdsourcing* and *crowdfunding*—that refer to a person's or organization's ability to reach the public to raise money, increase awareness, and create change on important social issues. Nonprofits that are smart, including churches, will realize we are watching the rise of a very cause-oriented generation. It's a generation that demands action in line with our words and effective change in light of real problems.

HopeMob founder Shaun King says:

> The ease of generosity through social media and online giving has proven itself to help the growth of generosity itself. People that previously had no idea of the difference they could make in the world have been emboldened by social media and are now aware of issues and needs and ways that they can provide solutions to them that just didn't exist decades ago.[2]

Today we know more about issues such as human trafficking and slavery, clean water, world hunger, genocide, persecution, and HIV/AIDS than ever before. This is a good thing. In the past whatever the government focused on got most of the attention of the media. This resulted in focus on problems in places where we had some particular political or economic interest. But with the rise of social media we're learning about huge problems in the rest of the world, and our worldviews are expanding rapidly as a result.

Generosity is not a value born in the social media age, but it's seeing a revival through it. It really began in the heart of God, the great giver. This is a God who gave His only Son for our sin, who gave the Holy Spirit to the church, who gives leaders to the world, who gave us a perfect revelation of Himself in Scripture, and who keeps giving His blessing daily to a world that often ignores Him.

REWIRING THE CHURCH WITH OLD VALUES

The church has an unprecedented opportunity to see revival in this social media age, not merely by talking about the need for revival online, but rather by recovering the values a social networking generation has made popular again. As I think through some of the values gaining attention in this social media economy, I can't help but reflect on the prevalence of these values in the early church.

Within the church we read about in the Book of Acts, we see a group of leaders who were willing to be authentically known as "ordinary men with no special training in the Scriptures...who had been with Jesus" (Acts 4:13). They spent time in each other's homes, endured persecution together, and spent long hours praying with one another. This early church was driven by the need for the gospel to circulate the globe in a passionate demonstration of others-centeredness. Granted, it took a wave of persecution to push them out of the comfort zone of their familiar home city, but once they began to move, they covered the earth with their teaching. And the early church was a model of generosity. In Jerusalem members of the church sold their extra property and pooled their money to provide homes and meals for those affected by a food supply shortage. The church took action to care for widows and orphans and spread good will alongside the gospel.

The church in our current culture needs sweeping change when it comes to some of these values. We must embody the message we preach with greater integrity, which often calls for a better balance between showing grace and upholding truth. We need to move away from tightly controlled institutional machinery to a more organic form of biblical community. We must acknowledge the problems of the world around us and rise to the occasion by doing something about those problems, putting feet to our prayers and making a tangible difference in society.

In a cause-oriented generation we serve the greatest cause of all! In a culture that demands authenticity, we have greater motivation to be authentic than any other kind of organization. In a time where being others-focused really stands out, we have the greatest motivation to care for others because of the gospel message. And in an age of generosity we have the potential to channel the financial resources of the church to effect real change in the world as never before.

None of these values are the result of a social media

revolution. They are the result of a revival of ideas originated in the mind and heart of God Himself and meant
for embodiment in the church.

Reflection and Discussion

1. What values do you see being talked about and promoted by leaders in the arena of social media that reflect values as old as the New Testament? What would you add?

2. In what ways does social media force us to be more authentic than ever? And in what ways can it contribute to inauthenticity?

3. What movements have you noticed taking off because of social media? What issues seem to get more attention now than in the era of mass communication, when media conglomerates set the tone for the conversation around social issues?

4. How does social media create the opportunity for a modern revival to take place? What needs to happen for us to see it come to pass?

Part II

BE SOCIAL. CHANGE
THE WORLD.

Chapter 6

TO EVERYTHING, THERE IS A PURPOSE

I 'VE ALWAYS ADMIRED trendsetters. It takes courage to be the first person to try something stupid that ends up working well for a large number of followers. I grew up in the 1980s, so I have deep admiration for the first rappers who wore huge white tennis shoes with no strings in them, the first ladies who went out in public with a six-inch-tall wall of bangs on their foreheads, and the first guy who "pegged" the legs of his blue jeans. I also know that, had I been the one to try any of those ideas, you would never have heard of any of them.

There is wisdom in observing what is happening around us and refusing to jump into every potential trend early on. If you, as a church leader, try to join every social network that introduces itself to the public, you're going to fry your brain. You can't keep up with every trend, and you can't be the first to adopt every new technology, and you shouldn't try to do so. When I consult with churches and organizations in the area of social media, I always advise them *not* to dive in headfirst without a purpose or a plan. It leads to failure, burnout, and a greater resistance to change in the future.

So, before you lead your church to adopt new forms of communication technologies, you need to answer one big question first: *Why?* Why are you starting a Facebook page? Why are you creating a

Twitter account? If you can't answer the question quickly, you have some homework to do first.

WRONG REASONS TO ADOPT NEW TECHNOLOGIES

I'm all about adopting new technologies, and I've written this entire book to encourage you to dive in. But before we do so, let's check our motives. There are some rather flawed reasons for adopting new tools that will set us up for problems later. Here are some reasons *not* to step into this brave new world.

Don't try something new because everyone else is doing it.

Leisure suits and butterfly collars pretty much prove this point, but I'll expand for the sake of making it clear. On the opposite end of the spectrum from the trendsetter is that last guy who's still clinging to something that went out of style a decade earlier. When churches do nothing but copy the cool kids, we wind up creating a Christian subculture that shows up to the table a decade late and does things only half as well as the original. It doesn't reflect well.

Case in point: I remember attending a conference for church creatives where Danny Yount was speaking. Danny is a video graphics whiz, an artist like few others. He created most of the video intros and special effects for the Iron Man movies, the Sherlock Holmes movies, and many others. You would recognize his work if you saw it. He's also a believer with a powerful testimony. And at the end of his talk to church creatives, he issued a final challenge: "Stop copying Hollywood. Be creative. Lead the world." If an amazing, talented artist with one foot in the church and one foot in Hollywood—one with a pretty legit reputation, no less—tells us we need to stop copying the culture, I think we'd be smart to listen. Don't you?

Don't try something new because no one else is doing it.

Nobody understands technology's influence on culture like Bobby Gruenewald and the team over at LifeChurch .tv. They reinvented the idea of Bible software, took it to the cloud, made it social, and changed the world by making the Scriptures more accessible and more popular than ever in history. Know how? They're the church that invented YouVersion—you know, that Bible app you probably installed on your phone ages ago and now use all the time? Yep. That was them.

But there's only one LifeChurch.tv. God may well have in mind for your church to lead in some area of innovation within the kingdom, but only a relative few will be so far out in front that they change the shape of modern evangelism. Forging ahead with the motive of being known as the first and the original usually leads to reinventing the wheel unsuccessfully. It wastes time and energy.

Don't try something new to fix deeper issues.

Who you are in the face-to-face world is who you should and will be in the world of online social media. For instance, if you struggle with relationships or leadership offline, you will probably struggle with it online too. Plunging into the world of social media will never fix the areas where you need improvement—and maybe even mentoring or training—in your church's daily life already. It will only highlight the very areas you're hoping it obscures.

WHY TO ENGAGE THE WORLD WITH SOCIAL MEDIA

As we develop a driving philosophy of why to take up the mantle of social media engagement, it's important to understand that the purposes for engaging the culture this way are the same purposes that led the church to engage with the world before the Internet ever existed.

We engage because the world needs Jesus.

Paul declared he would "try to find common ground with everyone, doing everything I can to save some" (1 Cor. 9:22). I don't think for a second Paul would ever have compromised the integrity of the theology he had carefully built while writing nearly half of the New Testament, but I do believe he was willing to adapt his communication style to any audience in order to be clear about the gospel. Paul's willingness to adapt to his surroundings was the outflow of a heart that broke for people who did not yet know Jesus.

The world needs Jesus, and the very people we want to reach with the gospel are involved in social media—especially those in the youngest generations. They're tweeting. They're Facebooking. They're Instagramming. We can't expect a lost world to come to our turf on our terms to hear our message. We must actively engage them with the hope that is in us. If we hope to share Jesus with them, we need to go where they already are.

We engage because the conversation happens with or without us.

Right now, people are talking about big issues. Dialogue is ongoing when it comes to politics, economics, science, medicine, sports, technology, and religion. In most areas of life someone is leading the conversation that's happening, and it isn't waiting for us to catch up. The conversation is happening whether we're a part of it or not.

In past centuries Christians have been willing to lead the conversation about art, science, and social issues. But within the last half-century our tendency has been to retreat into our Christian bubbles where everything feels comfortable to us. If we're honest, we'd rather spend time talking to other Christians about the Christian life than risk engaging in conversations with people who disagree with us or have tough questions we can't answer. It takes courage to engage, but engage we must if we are to lead the conversation about Jesus forward.

*We engage because God should be glorified
in every space.*

I remember Rick Warren talking about a conversation
he had with John Piper about Twitter. At the time Piper
had created a Twitter account but Rick had not. They
spoke at an event together, and Rick questioned Piper
about embracing a medium that, in Rick's thinking at
the time, dumbed down communication and fostered
narcissism. Piper responded that it is the responsibility
of Christians to fill every space with the glory of God—
even the online space. That conversation pushed Rick
into tweeting, and now he is one of the most influential
church figures using Twitter today.

In every space where people are talking, the glory of
God should be evident. His light should be shined into
the darkest corners of society. It stands to reason that
if the role of Twitter and other social networks is to
empower everyday people with a voice, then we should
certainly take advantage of the opportunity to use that
voice to point people to the glory of God.

*We engage because it's the mission of the
church.*

It is impossible to fulfill the Great Commission as
Jesus gave it without engaging the culture around us. The
members of the earliest church in the city of Jerusalem
would confirm this. Jesus had plainly commissioned them
to not only share the gospel with their surrounding community, but also to do so to the uttermost parts of the
earth. They did well locally, but they failed to leave their

city. So persecution came. What happened next? The Bible says that "the believers who were scattered preached the Good News about Jesus wherever they went" (Acts 8:4). They had to learn the lesson the hard way that God is serious about us going to every piece of the planet with the good news.

Obviously social media won't help us reach every people group left in the world. Many do not have access to electricity, much less the Internet. But the online world does give us a window into an ever-widening portion of the world's population. And the United Nations, on June 3, 2011, declared Internet access to be a basic human right: "Given that the Internet has become an indispensable tool for realizing a range of human rights, combating inequality, and accelerating development and human progress, ensuring universal access to the Internet should be a priority for all states."[1] Corporations and governments are seeking ways to extend the reach of the Internet to everyone. In other words, more roads are being paved for the church to complete its mission.

We engage because people need us to engage.

Why does the United Nations consider access to the Internet a basic human right? Because the world's leading thinkers understand the Internet is a virtually limitless source of knowledge updated in real time. Living conditions can be improved by giving people access to knowledge about anything from better architecture to advanced medical training to new farming methods and more.

And then there's the fact that in every country in the

world there is a church. It may be small and underground, but churches exist virtually everywhere. The Internet affords churches access to this massive infrastructure for helping mankind. Even in impoverished nations church leaders tend to gather to discuss the needs of their respective congregations. Some places have no hospitals or grocery stores, but there are churches. These churches, with the aid of the Internet, can help to serve and lead their communities.

Imagine the results we could see if we really used social media to meet the needs of people, not only in places where the Internet is just now becoming available but also in our own backyards. When I was at Saddleback Church, I sat in on numerous conversations about how to "do church" online. We tackled the typical questions about whether the service should be a live stream or recorded, what technological systems to use for content delivery, and how to track involvement. One day my boss, David, asked an important question: "How can we give 'a cup of cold water in Jesus's name' online?" In other words, is there a way for Christians to serve one another and the world at large over the Internet?

Serving others online is not as hard as you might think. Obviously you can't build a wheelchair ramp or grow a crop online (FarmVille doesn't count!), but it is possible to counsel and pray with people about their problems over social networks, through e-mail, via blogs, and in chat formats. People have real needs that can be met via social media. Therefore, social media is a tool that cannot be ignored as a viable means of extending the Great

Commission and helping others heal with the message of Jesus.

There's a purpose for everything under heaven. This means that there's a purpose for the Internet, and there also ought to be purpose in the way that we use it. You may be tempted to think, "Everyone's using the Internet, and people keep telling us we need to use the Internet too. Let's go!" In that thinking, you may be additionally tempted to just jump in. Resist this urge, at least for the moment. Keep reading and learning about these tools that are available, and keep thinking about how you can use them on your own or with your unique staff and community to suit your unique purpose and calling. Take care to use these tools with purpose.

Reflection and Discussion

1. How does the church sometimes fail in its intended purpose when it tries to do what no one else is doing without enough forethought and planning?

2. In what ways do you see churches embracing things that are trendy without contextualizing new methods to their own respective mission fields?

3. Having read the reasons why we engage the present culture through social technologies, why is it crucial that churches embrace this wave and stay current?

4. What reason for engaging the world using social media most compels you?

Chapter 7

I N A RECENT conversation with some other church-planting leaders, I was asked what I see as the greatest weaknesses in evangelicalism today. There are plenty to identify, but the one I feel most strongly about is the lack of confidence I see in some of the brightest of leaders. Like a sleeping giant, today's church leaders have the potential to triumph over some of the world's biggest problems if they would only realize it. In a sort of false humility we convince ourselves that quietness is the path to godliness.

One of the reasons I believe the church has been slow to adopt social media as a tool in our ministry arsenal is because of our perception that it feeds narcissism—a legitimate concern I will address below. We try to guard against creating a celebrity culture within Christianity, and since social media has the real potential to inflate egos and magnify individual personalities, we are perhaps so careful that we fail to capitalize on its benefits.

The greatest resource at our disposal in the realm of social media isn't Facebook or Twitter. It isn't any mobile device or tablet. It's *you*. One of my favorite definitions of *preaching* is from Phillips Brooks, who described preaching as "the communication of divine truth through a man to men."[1] The historical fact is that God has always chosen to use unique, individual personalities to communicate on His behalf to every generation.

GOD USES PEOPLE

Fifteen years ago I was in a conference for pastors where John Greene was speaking, and he made a point I'd never considered before. He stated simply, "God doesn't bless a church or an organization. He blesses a man." Pastor Greene's words could be quite controversial. We are all too familiar with pastors who've gone on power trips and have allowed their pride to dominate and destroy their ministries. It's always possible that a leader could wind up building more of a personal empire of popularity than a genuine platform for the spreading of the gospel.

But John was right.

When God spoke through Ezekiel about the broken condition of Israel, he announced, "And I sought a man among them who should build up the wall and stand in the gap before Me for the land, that I should not destroy it, but I found none" (Ezek. 22:30, AMP). The Bible is replete with examples of this principle.

When God wanted to form for Himself a nation of people who would bring honor and glory to Himself, He called Abraham out of Ur. From that one man He initiated the generations of all of the Jews who ever lived. When He wanted to save that same struggling nation during a massive worldwide famine, He raised up Joseph from the pit and the prison to the palace, where he would become the second most powerful man on the planet.

After four hundred years of Egyptian slavery God found Moses in the wilderness and equipped him to confront Pharaoh and lead the people of Israel to freedom in the Promised Land. Then it was Joshua who commanded the nation's military as they marched into Canaan in victory over the land's inhabitants. The Book of Judges is a chronicle of the men and women God used to sustain the life of the Israelites during a time of shifting values and moral decay.

A Moabitess named Ruth became a life-saving instrument in God's hands when she married Boaz and continued the family lineage of Jesus. Between the period of the judges and the era of the kings, God used a humble prophet named Samuel to lead and guide His people. Samuel would become a bridge between two phases of life for Israel and would pour the anointing oil on both Saul and David. And it was David whom God used to establish Jerusalem as the capital of the nation of Israel and to devote four decades of his life to winning battles to secure the peace of the people. Solomon was the man God called and used to establish a place of worship by building the temple in Jerusalem.

Then, during the Assyrian captivity, Esther was sovereignly placed in the king's court for "such as time as this" (Esther 4:4) when an ancient Hitler-figure named Haman sought to annihilate God's people. Between the empires of Assyria and Babylon God used the often eccentric personalities of prophets such as Isaiah, Ezekiel, Jeremiah, and Daniel to speak words of both comfort and warning to a people under persecution and in a position of judgment.

God used John the Baptist to prepare the way for the Messiah to begin His anointed ministry, and He obviously used Jesus to provide a sacrificial atonement for the sins of humanity. Jesus called, trained, and later restored a fallen apostle Peter along with John and James to help launch a world-changing movement of God called the church. And He knocked a Roman official off his horse and blinded him into humble recognition of Jesus as Lord so that He could use the apostle Paul as a pioneering missionary church planter to spread the message of the gospel all over the Mediterranean world.

Church history continues to detail God's choice of men and women for His special tasks for the last two centuries. The space and scope of this present volume doesn't afford me the liberty of detailing the biographies of some of my greatest personal heroes, but they include Polycarp, Athanasius, John Chrysostom, and St. Augustine; Hubmaier, Wycliffe, Calvin, Luther, and Wesley; Charles Spurgeon, D. L. Moody, Hudson Taylor, and Adoniram Judson. My own life has been heavily influenced by more modern giants such as Adrian Rogers, W. A. Criswell, Rick Warren, Warren Wiersbe, and Charles Swindoll.

There is no denying this one basic fact: when God wants to launch a movement, save a nation, or change a culture, He raises up individuals whom He fills with His Spirit for the special purpose to which they are called. It happens in neighborhoods, small towns, college classes, wings of government, and workplaces of every kind. And God wants to use you!

Excuses, Excuses

God once appeared to a man in the form of a burning bush and spoke audibly to him with a special assignment to go free a nation of people from slavery. Though Moses was familiar with God's voice and certainly astounded by the sight of the bush, his inclination was to say, "I'm probably not the right guy, Lord." And believers have been honoring Moses's tradition of making excuses to escape God's calling ever since.

When I talk to church leaders about engaging in social media, I hear some of the same excuses for not doing so over and over again.

"I don't have time for social media."

This particular excuse is almost always motivated by a misperception. Leaders have in their minds the image of a recluse cooped up in an office behind a computer, spending hours on end browsing Twitter and commenting on Facebook. Social media is often perceived as an activity that needs to be added to an already busy schedule.

But this simply isn't the case.

Yes, effectively using social media adds some extra activity to your schedule, but not in the way you might think. I, for one, consider myself fairly well engaged in the social-networking world. As of this writing I've sent almost thirty-five thousand tweets. In the minds of many such an accomplishment must have taken me thousands of hours, cumulatively speaking. But the fact is, I didn't sit behind a computer and think up thirty-five thousand different things to say on Twitter. More than half of those are merely links to articles I've read and found interesting. While reading an article on my phone or my laptop, I click a single button and share it with my Twitter audience. Another significant portion of those tweets have been replies to people in a conversation. Many are photos I've snapped with my phone and shared with friends online in a matter of seconds.

You could reasonably engage in a fair amount of social media activity in fifteen to thirty minutes per day—not all at once, but spread over the course of simply doing life as you normally do it. Social media, by its nature, integrates well into the schedule and routine you've already set for yourself. It merely requires some intentionality and some setup on your part.

I also believe social media is rapidly becoming a normal means of communication. I use Facebook's messaging feature almost as much as I use e-mail to communicate with friends. Eventually avoiding social media will be akin to choosing not to have a mailbox.

This particular excuse also flows out of a false understanding of value. We assume social media has little relational value and therefore shouldn't compete with the activities we're already involved in, which we perceive to be far more important. But I can testify to the life-changing power of social media. Some of the relationships that have been most vital to my life and ministry have been initiated online.

I met David Chrzan, Saddleback Church's chief of staff, through Twitter and later joined the church's staff as a pastor. I met Derwin Gray through Twitter as well. Derwin has coached me and supported our new church plant financially and prayerfully as our relationship has developed. I met Artie Davis through Twitter and later began speaking for Artie at the conferences he was facilitating about leading churches in small towns. And the list goes on.

Your time is valuable, so investing it wisely probably means engaging in social media, not avoiding it.

"I don't want to act like a celebrity."

Then don't. As a matter of fact, the more you act like a celebrity, the less effective you'll be at social media. Granted, social media makes people more visible to the rest of the world, but being visible isn't always the same as taking center stage. Celebrities are known by many but intimately known by few. Their names are recognizable, but their personas are only as knowable as their press. What really sets celebrities apart from the rest of us is the exclusivity that surrounds them. They simply aren't as accessible as the rest of us.

The beautiful side of social media is that it demands we get personable—that we be accessible. Avoid the celebrity mentality by joining in a two-way conversation rather than simply broadcasting into the air. This is a must if we're going to communicate to real people about real issues.

Furthermore, it's undeniable that God uses the power of personalities, even of celebrities, to drive entire movements. Earlier I mentioned a few names of reformers. Their names are remembered for a reason: God uses individuals to lead movements. You may not want to be a self-centered celebrity (and I'm glad you don't!), but I do hope you desire God to use you for significant impact—to fuel a movement either as its leader or a primary enthusiast. We need courageous men and women to speak up.

"I'm just not into technology."

Neither are most of the people actively joining the conversation around you. Technology nuts tend to be the earliest adopters of tools that later become a normal part of the lives of everyone else. When I joined Twitter, it was primarily because of my interest in web development. I found myself networking with graphic designers, front-end web developers, and bloggers. Initially Twitter seemed like a small galaxy in a larger Internet universe.

Then everyone else started joining.

Internet marketers jumped in fairly quickly, since social media has the potential to spread a message far and fast. News outlets realized Twitter was the fastest way to break news. Then major household brands, from soft drinks to underwear, jumped into the arena to improve their images. Celebrities joined next, and then everyone else. Technologists might have been first, but now they make up the minority of social media users.

My ten-year-old daughter, Ella, has an iPod with games, music, pictures, and messaging capabilities. And my two-year-old son, Sam, struggles to put sentences together, but he's an Angry Birds champion. My point is, you don't have to be a computer programmer anymore. You just have to know how to swipe a finger across a little screen. Social media ceased to be about the technology a few years ago. Now the fastest-growing segment of Facebook users isn't young computer geeks spending their time in coffee shops but fifty-five- to sixty-four-year-old women[2]—grandmas who want to connect and see pictures of their grandkids.

"I don't know where to begin."

Good. We're getting there. In the next chapter we'll talk about how to jump into the conversation, and in the final part of the book I'll offer some rapid-fire suggestions and tips for utilizing the major tools available for social media today. But just in case you haven't already, head over to Twitter.com, Facebook.com, and LinkedIn.com and sign up.

When Vince Lombardi became the coach of the Green Bay Packers, he took a bunch of pride-filled pros and brought them back to the basics. "Everybody stop and gather around," he said. Then he knelt down, picked up the pigskin, and said, "Let's start at the beginning. This is a football. These are the yard markers. I'm the coach. You are the players."[3]

As I noted in the previous chapter, there is certainly a time to apply the breaks and go slowly as you understand what you're getting into a little better. But don't wait forever. There comes a time when it's necessary to get started.

"I don't like attention."

Hey, I get it. I'm an introvert. I had to give an oral book report in the sixth grade and nearly threw up preparing for it. I'm only a teaching pastor by the grace and enabling of God. I don't like attention any more than you do. I'd rather just blend.

But a decade and a half ago I wrestled with a calling from God in which He asked me to stand up and share the gospel. I said yes because I believe God can use anyone. Furthermore He *wants* to use everyone—including you.

STAND UP AND BE NOTICED

God uses the good news of Jesus to change the world, and He communicates that good news through the medium of human personalities. So it stands to reason that God wants to use your personality in communicating the gospel to others, and social media is an arena where our unique individual personalities shine.

In other words, it's time to stand up and be counted. But as you step forward, there are some important guiding principles to remember.

Be the real you.

The rapid rise of social media in our culture has had some significant positive effects. One such effect is the raised expectation of authenticity. Yes, it's easy to be fake in the world of social media, but getting caught has higher stakes and quicker fallout than ever.

Our lives are more transparent than ever before. It takes seconds for reputations to be ruined. The lesson? Be real. Be you.

I know what some of you are thinking: "Can God use ordinary me?" Absolutely! In fact, it is your uniqueness, even down to the subtle nuances of your personality that you might not like, that draws others to you. God wired us to be in fellowship with others, so we're naturally drawn to people who allow us to know the real them. The same is true of you. People will line up to know the real you. I'm challenging you to be the real you online.

Welcome healthy attention.

You would most likely say you don't like attention, right? But not liking attention is no excuse for disengaging from the culture. Imagine if Jesus had rejected opportunities to have attention focused on Him. The crowds would not have been taught, fed, healed, or persuaded to follow Him. He might have avoided the cross and resurrection as well. But Jesus had a healthy sense of mission, or "sent-ness," and therefore He embraced attention as a means of sharing truth.

The online world is certainly cluttered with all kinds of people grabbing attention in all the wrong ways. Some have had meltdowns on social media only to have to close their accounts in embarrassment later. Others have spent their time spamming and sending unwanted and unsolicited sales pitches to innocent people. There is definitely a danger in going overboard in using shock value to get a message across. And after the shock is over, there are often negative repercussions.

But for every healthy means of attracting attention, there is a healthy alternative to be employed. Mark Horvath is one of the best examples I know of a guy who knows how to attract positive attention online, and he uses it for tremendous good. He's the mind behind invisiblepeople.tv—an online video blog that brings attention to the issue of homelessness through interviews with homeless people—and if Mark ever rubs someone the wrong way, it's almost always because his passion for the homeless is so intense. He's not afraid to travel into the worst neighborhoods on the planet to film and spread the stories of homeless people. It's attention-getting, and it's a ministry God is using for good.

You too can attract healthy attention by producing great material, adopting and championing a cause, helping people unexpectedly, genuinely encouraging someone, and being an example of generosity.

Be a bright spot.

In the world in which we live, everybody is in need of a bright spot in the day. We live in somewhat of a good news vacuum, and everyone needs encouragement. Couple society's need for good news with the biblical responsibility given to believers to encourage one another, and you can see how a ministry of online encouragement is a tremendous opportunity for good. Think about the big impact of little phrases such as "Keep up the good work," "Hang in there," "Praying for you," and "Rooting for you." It doesn't take much, but the minimum requirement is a commitment to showing up.

Are there concerns about social media that need to be considered? Sure, as there are with any new technological development, but most of the concerns we have explored in recent years within the social media environment have turned out to be unfounded. The benefits of engaging, especially in terms of reaching people with the gospel, far outweigh the negatives.

When God provides a tool, He expects us to use it for His glory and for the redemption of His people. And amazingly He wants to use you and your unique personality and your circle of social influence to fulfill the Great Commission. You matter to His mission far more than you know.

Reflection and Discussion

1. God uses people to accomplish His will. Why, then, are we so careful not to assert ourselves as influencers? Why does the idea of developing a "personal brand" make us so nervous as Christians?

2. Of the categories of excuses that are highlighted by Moses's experience, which most directly hits home with you? What excuses do you think you've made for using social media to spread the gospel?

3. Why do we find it such a challenge to let people around us see the "real" us? How can we cultivate greater personal authenticity in our relationships with others?

4. God wants to use you to encourage others. Whom can you encourage today or in the next week, and how will you do so?

Chapter 8

JUMP IN. JOIN THE CONVERSATION.

I N OUR MOST recent presidential election between Barack Obama and Mitt Romney, President Obama won by quite a wide margin, at least in electoral votes. Both presidential hopefuls entered the campaign season enthusiastically, and both candidates kept up their confidence to the very end. But the Obama campaign had reason to be a little more confident than its opponent. Regardless of where you stand politically, it must be admitted that Obama's team was keenly aware of the power of social media in a way the Romney team could never quite grasp.

By the end of the election President Obama's Facebook page had more than thirty-one million "likes," compared to Romney's ten million. On Twitter, the president had twenty-one million followers while Romney had just a million and a half. And President Obama had more than ten times as many YouTube subscribers.

Do the numbers of followers and subscribers necessarily indicate who will win an election? Certainly not, but they are a hint.

What is more telling, however, is the way each campaign chose to engage the conversation happening online. During the second presidential debate, for example, the Obama team sent a total of thirty-seven tweets. The Romney team? Two. And as of a week before the election, Obama had three times as many Facebook fans as Romney, ten times as many YouTube subscribers, and twelve times as many Twitter followers.[1] One team joined the conversation happening within our culture more effectively than the other, and it happened to be the team that won the election.

The Conversation Is Happening

Have you ever had that weird feeling that people across the room are talking about you, even though you can't tell what they're saying? It's a little spooky, and it's true of most brands and organizations. It's also true of Christianity, of your denomination, and of your church. Conversations are occurring all the time whether we join them or not. There are now thousands of tweets posted *every second* on Twitter. People are talking loudly, quickly, and often. Trying to keep up with the collective, real-time updates of a few hundred people is like trying to scoop the Nile River into a plastic cup.

Given that reality, leaders in the social-networking industry have figured out ways to make the conversation digestible. Consider the power of the hashtag (represented by the # sign), the proliferation of news aggregation sites, and the major shift Facebook has made from showing you every update about your friends to showing you only that which has the most relevance to your life (at least according to Facebook).

When someone is new to the world of social media, they usually ask something such as, "How in the world do you keep up with everyone you follow?" This reflects the mentality that everything deserves response, like a phone call. But I like to think of social networks more like party lines. Remember when Andy Griffith needed to place a phone call? He would pick up the phone and ask Sarah, the operator, to get someone on the line. Usually, however, Aunt Bea's friends were already tying up the line with a group conversation. Mayberry had one line, and everybody shared it.

Twitter, Facebook, and other emerging networks are like party lines. Pick up the receiver at any time to tune into the stream of conversation. Dip in here or there and get just a taste. Track the topics that interest you. Follow the people who intrigue you. Take in only as much as you can process and then hang up. It's fairly acceptable to jump into almost any conversation that happens online as long as you know enough of the context to make sense when you speak up.

So, with all this conversation happening, how can we possibly engage in a good way? I'm glad you asked.

Get to know people.

Following someone and observing the content they produce is no longer considered stalking. It's called education. It's also a way of making an introduction. About once per day I glance to see who has followed me on Twitter, not because I desire popularity but to discover interesting people. Granted, some are spammers and others aren't human at all (those are called robots or spambots, and yes, that's a real thing), but there are usually a few people I haven't met who share a lot in common with me.

Following someone's updates lets them know you're interested in what they have to say. And in the world of social media being *interested* is just as important as being *interesting*—if not more important. When we tune into the lives of the people around us, we have the opportunity for real influence.

David Chrzan, Saddleback's chief of staff, once showed me an acronym based on the word SPEAK as a reminder for how to walk through a conversation with someone you wish to know better:

- What's your **story**?

- What's your **passion**?

- How can I **encourage** you?

- **Ask,** how can I help you?

- Whom do you **know** whom I should know?

This kind of curiosity and genuine interest makes a real difference to people—both online and off. Right? People just want to know you care. Get to know them, and show them you do.

Track the conversations that matter to you.

Since you can't listen to everything, it's important to be able to tune into the conversations that matter most to you. For instance, I was once speaking to Saddleback

Church's staff about using Twitter. While speaking, I was also projecting on the screen a monitored search for every tweet using the phrase "pray for" within a one hundred mile radius of Orange County, California. (You can do this under Twitter's advanced search features.) As I was speaking, we noticed that a new tweet popped up from a gentleman in Los Angeles who was asking for prayer while on his way to court for a crime. Glancing at his previous tweets revealed he was most likely involved in gang-related crime.

Our staff stopped and prayed for the man, and I sent him a message on the spot about how Rick Warren and the staff of Saddleback Church were stopping to pray for him. I also asked him to follow up with us to let us know how his court appearance went. He immediately replied with a big thank-you, and the next day he indeed updated us on his day in court, which apparently turned out well for him.

There is power in listening to the right conversations and chiming in at the right times. I use Twitter's "lists" feature to keep lists of people in various industries—publishing, pastoral ministry, and social media, to name a few. At any time I wish, I can view the tweets from any one of those lists exclusively, and I love the chance to tune in and contribute to conversations happening in real time on my subjects of interest.

LinkedIn is a particularly powerful solution for tuning into conversations as well, but they happen off the beaten path on that network in something called "groups." Granted, many LinkedIn groups are little more than bulletin boards used for the regurgitation of links already shared all over the Internet elsewhere. But in groups you're introduced to people with similar interests and common connections. Whatever industry you might find yourself working in, LinkedIn most likely has several groups that can help to condense a stream of information into a channel tailored to what you really want to know about.

One other tool that deserves mention when it comes to tracking conversations online is Google Alerts. When you're logged into your Google account, do a search for something and then notice an option on the screen to save the search as a Google Alert. Once you've saved the search, you'll have the option to receive a daily digest of new mentions that crop up online on your topic of choice. These alerts let you spot new information quickly about any subject, enabling you, for example, to catch complaints and criticisms as well as praise and positive testimonials people make about your church. There are times when both kinds of mentions deserve responses, and since you'll be tuning in to the conversation, you'll be able to provide just such a response when needed.

Contribute value to the conversation.

Listening matters a great deal. In fact, a good rule of thumb is to listen at least twice as much as you speak, not only in the world of social media but also in all of your relationships. But joining the conversation requires that at some point you respond with a valuable contribution of your own. This goes back to the basic idea of having the courage to speak up, and the world definitely needs your voice.

Now our task is not necessarily to create the conversation. Again the conversation is already happening. It's stimulated by shifts in the economy, the political landscape, new technological developments, and other surprising events of all shapes and sizes. Our task is certainly not to control the conversation, either, though that is often our comfort zone. We tend to want the world to talk about subjects that matter to us, and we feel more at ease when we're addressing questions for which we have easy answers, even if those questions aren't being asked by anyone.

Our real task is to just join the conversation, which means building up trust equity and earning a hearing with people. Few people have a better handle on this than Chris Garrett, one of the leaders on the social web, who writes:

> More and more we are turning to people who have something useful to share, who our friends trust, and who can prove they get results. If you want credibility that is what you need to start doing. Share your best tips, your case studies, and interact with people in a live setting.[2]

Providing value begins with being trustworthy and proving our integrity. The authority that really matters the most is our moral authority. When it comes to sharing the gospel, a skeptical world will be asking the tough question, "Do you even have a right to talk about this? If you claim that Jesus can change my life, can you first prove that He's changed *your* life?"

Honesty isn't the *best* policy. It's the *only* policy that works.

Take the lead.

The church has, historically, had good experiences leading cultural conversations, but we've slipped behind in the last century or so. Most of the great educational institutions in the West can trace their beginnings to a church or denomination. Many of them left their religious roots long ago, but their histories prove that the church has been willing to lead cultural conversations in the past, even beyond the realm of religion.

Real leaders are rarely obnoxious. They are typically not the know-it-alls in the room or the show-offs. But they are confident in their ability to lead. Real conversation leaders are willing to take the risk of being wrong to make a good point. They listen to the input of others. And they understand that everyone should benefit from the collective wisdom of everyone else.

This is not a challenge to start talking to avoid silence. The results of speaking without thinking are almost always disastrous. It is instead a challenge to take the leap and join in. Join Twitter. Log into Facebook again. Join a group on LinkedIn. Speak into the vacuum that is our culture. If you're a believer in Jesus, then you have the authority of God's perfect Word, the assurance of God's presence, and the collective wisdom of a couple thousand years of church history guiding and supporting you. The world most definitely needs what you have to say whether you realize it or not. So jump in. Join the conversation, and stick with it no matter how awkward it may feel at first.

Reflection and Discussion

1. What are some of the biggest conversations taking place in the culture around you right now? What is the media talking about? Where is the church's voice in these conversations?

2. Conversations are more public than ever. People dialogue with other individuals in front of the entire watching public on social networks. How can you join in the conversations that are happening without coming across as prying?

3. In what ways are you currently analyzing your effectiveness in communicating online? How do you keep track of your audience and manage conversations? How could you improve in this area?

4. Think about the leaders you know online who tend to lead conversations. What can you learn from them? What can you do to set the stage for discussion online?

D ID YOU KNOW there are an estimated one hundred million land mines to be found in at least seventy countries around the world, according to OneWorld International? Since the mid-1970s land mines have killed or maimed more than one million people, which has led to a worldwide effort to ban further land mine use and get rid of existing land mines.[1]

The trouble with land mines lies in their intent. They are devices designed to remain hidden and to explode unexpectedly in the face of an unsuspecting enemy. Obviously, however, they usually hurt innocent people.

It would be irresponsible to write a book urging people to adopt social technologies without also being honest about some of the inherent dangers in doing so. But first let me clarify a very important point: technology is amoral. The computer is not the Antichrist, the Internet is not illegal, and electricity has not corrupted us all. But every new technological tool has the potential to be used in both moral and immoral ways.

Among the objections I often hear to churches being involved in the social media arena is that social media is dangerous. Usually someone will refer anecdotally to a person who has initiated an extramarital affair over a social network, and so they will, in turn, write off any legitimate use of social networking for ministry purposes. But if this line of reasoning is followed to its conclusion, churches should take down their websites from an Internet where pornography exists. We should kill Christian television programming since it lies alongside shows that glorify crime and sexual immorality. And it would be a good idea to stop printing Christian books since some publishers print materials that promote evil and condemn Christianity.

The medium isn't guilty. The messengers are.

Put Your Guard Up

So what does this mean? It means that we need to live in reality: anytime we engage in new communication opportunities, we open the door to trouble, either through our ignorance or willful choice. And in the spirit of guarding our hearts against evil, it's important to be aware of the potential land mines that exist online. Let's explore the big ones.

We need to guard our eyes online.

Pornography has been around a lot longer than the Internet, but the Internet has made it more affordable, more accessible, and more anonymous to access than ever before. In other words, the Internet doesn't force anyone to sin, but it makes sin much easier for sinners. There are plenty of statistical studies about how many people are dabbling in or addicted to online pornography, but what is more alarming is that so many Christians believe that it's fairly harmless. The destroyed relationships in its wake tell a different story.

Ultimately pornography decreases a user's interest in reality and causes them to be satisfied with nothing less than the fantasy they've watched and stored in their minds. According to FightTheNewDrug.org, more than 50 percent of Internet pornography viewers admit to losing interest in deepening their relationships with a loved one. About 56 percent of divorces involve at least one spouse having an obsessive interest in pornography. And pornography increases the marital infidelity rate by more than 300 percent![2]

It's undeniable that pornography lurks just a click or two away from any Internet user. And there are no perfect devices for protection. Filters can be fooled, and firewalls can be penetrated. Craig Gross and his team at XXXChurch.com have released what are probably the most helpful tools available. In addition to filtering software, they offer a product designed for online accountability that will send a history of any questionable sites a person visits to a group of preselected friends. They also offer online help for pornography addiction recovery.

We need to guard our hearts online.

Facebook has earned a reputation for being a relationship wrecking ball. But like any other tool, I would maintain that the medium is neutral, but the users determine whether it's used for good or ill. However, it can't be disputed that social networking is a real part of the story for many relationships that have fallen apart. According to ABC News, "A third of all divorce filings in 2011 contained the word 'Facebook,' and more than 80 percent of U.S. divorce attorneys say social networking in divorce proceedings is on the rise, according to Divorce Online and the American Academy of Matrimonial Lawyers, respectively."[3] Why has social networking been such a problem for married people? Because it's amazingly intuitive when it comes to reconnecting us to old acquaintances and almost as skilled at connecting us with new acquaintances with whom we share many common interests. When we feel our needs are not being met within our marriages, we create a false sense of reality and believe that rekindling an old flame or sparking a new one will fill the void. As in the case of the problem of pornography, it's still about our selfishness and sinfulness at the core.

Our hearts are vulnerable, especially in these online mediums, and we need to be careful to guard them and keep them pure.

We need to guard our tongues online.

Alec Baldwin's meltdown on an airplane from having to turn off his cell phone in the middle of an important game of Words With Friends was talked about within minutes. Other rants by celebrities have been thoroughly documented as well. The fact is, anger rarely comes across well in 140 characters or less. Our adoring public never has the context of our emotions or the facial and physical cues that would normally help complete the story. Whether we intend the damage or not, it's quite possible for a ministry or professional reputation to be destroyed in a matter of seconds due to an ill-advised status update.

We need to find a way to be careful about walking the line between being transparent and being misunderstood. It takes seconds to post an update but much longer to embrace the consequences and repercussions of those few seconds and few words we transmitted across the Internet in a moment of poor judgment.

We need to guard our message online.

I believe social media and freedom go hand in hand. Sitting in church pews around the world are millions of believers who are already networking online, just waiting for a mandate from church leaders to go into the online world and preach the gospel. But releasing a volunteer army of that magnitude will also create some confusion along the way. Someone will most certainly misrepresent us and our message.

One of my roles at Saddleback Church during my year as a pastor there was to lead the Correspondence Team. The team was made up of several awesome ladies who did a tremendous job responding to thousands of e-mails in conjunction with a dozen and a half volunteers. We were committed to responding to everyone we possibly could, whether we had a good answer for them or not.

I learned in that role that some rumors never die. We answered some questions about Saddleback Church and Rick Warren repeatedly and even came up with templates that the volunteers could use when answering them.

When Rick Warren tweets, people listen. Often his

tweets would stir people to send an e-mail asking for clarification. When a new issue arose, our team would meet together and discuss the response. It was vitally important that we remain in agreement and that we represent Rick's views accurately, regardless of what the masses might say.

If you help your church in the realm of social media (and if you're reading this book, chances are you should be doing so), talk with your leaders about the central themes of your church's teachings. Formulate a list of frequently asked questions, and be sure that the leadership is in agreement on how to respond to questions. You may not be able to control every tweet or post from your membership, but you can be ready when questions arise.

We need to guard others online.

Conflict is a part of life, as is criticism. As we mature, both in age and in spiritual completeness, we should be learning how to deal with both in healthy ways. If we aren't prepared to handle conflict and criticism in a constructive manner, social media can be a nasty trap.

The temptation will always be there to use our social networking prowess in a competitive manner against those who might criticize us or with whom we have conflict. But the Bible has very clear guidelines for our behavior in this area. Paul said, "Get rid of all bitterness, rage, anger, harsh words, and slander, as well as all types of evil behavior. Instead, be kind to each other, tenderhearted, forgiving one another, just as God through Christ has forgiven you" (Eph. 4:31–32).

It's a good idea, therefore, to decide on your standards

for online behavior. Many companies have written entire social media policies so their employees know what will and will not be tolerated in their interactions with the public. And just as an employee is a continual representative of a company, so a Christian is a forever ambassador for the King. We need to guard our egos online.

Just as weeds must be killed at their roots, most bad behaviors must be killed at the point of our egos. Online social networks have a tendency to foster an atmosphere of positivity that encourages empty flattery, which doesn't exactly help our sinful nature to stay dead and out of the way. And pride, of course, is the source of all kinds of evil attitudes and behaviors. How does one keep the ego in check, online or off?

First, remember that it's not about you. It's about God. It's always been about God. God created us for a God-centered life, not a self-centered one. His purpose for you is to return His love—that's worship. And His purpose for social media is that He might be glorified as more people come to know Him—that's evangelism. Maintaining a right posture in social media means a daily evaluation of why we're spending our time online. Is it for ourselves? Or is it for Him?

Second, remember God's grace. I once invited a friend of mine to come teach a series of messages at the church I was leading. When he got to town, we met him at a fairly nice hotel and got him into his room. He dropped his bags in the lobby, looked up at the large chandelier, and with sincerity exclaimed, "Wow, I deserve hell, and I'm staying here!" I learned a lot from that statement, and

I've never forgotten it. I am not what others might think I am. I am simply who I am in Christ.

Third, die to criticism. Ego can keep us from hearing constructive criticism, but it can also cause us to obsess about it. When pride takes over, we develop a sense of "how dare they question the great and powerful *me*?" When criticism and disagreement come, even online, we should practice the discipline of not having to have the last word.

Fourth, die to praise. If there is a greater threat to our God-centered self-image than criticism, it's praise. In the realm of social media flattery is inevitable. Die to it. Let it roll off your back just as you might an unfairly harsh word. Another of my favorite phrases I've often repeated over the years is "Let's just blame that on Jesus."

And finally, put others first. Jesus set the example here, and Paul wrote to the Philippians reminding them of His approach to life:

> Don't be selfish; don't try to impress others. Be humble, thinking of others as better than your-selves. Don't look out only for your own interests, but take an interest in others, too.
> —Philippians 2:3–4

Are You Willing to Risk It?

Could something go wrong if we decide to engage the world in social networking? Absolutely. Should we then keep quiet and withdraw into a shell to hide? Absolutely not!

As I was writing this chapter, I was engaging in a conversation in an online group about the role of social media in the church. A question arose about whether churches should encourage or discourage the use of cell phones in church. I shared that at Grace Hills Church, we show a slide at the beginning of every service telling people, "Please turn your cell phones ON." We ask people to check in on Facebook, use our bulletin's mobile version as well as the online communication form, and then to post their thoughts publicly during the message.

The response to my sharing this approach was unexpected. One leader spoke of the irreverence of typing on a phone during church services. Another was concerned people would be distracted with social networking and texting. But as we've covered several times in this book already, the conversation goes on with or without us. People will be texting and tweeting in church whether we like it or not. Perhaps there is power in engaging them and joining the conversation in spite of the potential land mines we will deal with along the way.

Reflection and Discussion

1. What do you see as the most dangerous land mines as leaders become more involved in social media? What are the issues you hear the most about?

2. What safeguards do you or your organization have in place to help protect the testimonies of leaders online?

3. How can ego become the worst threat of all when it comes to social media engagement? How do you keep your own ego in check?

4. Is engaging the culture online worth the risk of facing the land mines mentioned in this chapter? If so, why?

Part III

THE "HOW" OF SOCIAL MEDIA

O N December 17, 1997, Jorn Barger coined the term "weblog" to describe a list of links he had visited and then posted on his website, Robot Wisdom.[1] And on that day blogging was born. In the beginning of blogging, most weblogs/blogs were like Jorn's—collections of links visited. But soon blogging became more.

Early bloggers developed two primary kinds of blogs: personal diaries or journals and independent opinion columns. Today there are tens of millions of active blogs, and nobody has an accurate count anymore.

Because of the way blogging began, it took a good decade for blogging to be recognized as legitimate writing, much less publishing. Now most blogging engines power magazine-like websites and offer the capacity for media-rich web content. Obviously most independent bloggers will never have the staffing power of a major news outlet or the connections necessary to break the world's biggest stories. But bloggers have become an influential bunch of people in their own right.

My own blogging journey began in 2004, when I started writing a brief weekly word to my congregation. I eventually moved those early articles to a new platform and started blogging more often and to a wider audience. In 2009 I was invited to become the

YOU ARE A PUBLISHER, LIKE IT OR NOT

editor of *Fuel Your Blogging*, a magazine about blogging published by the Fuel Creative Group based in New York. My experience with the Fuel team afforded me numerous opportunities to connect with successful bloggers, writers, and creatives. I had the privilege of interacting with bloggers whose followings are some of the largest in the industry.

And I became convinced that the church, on the whole, should be blogging.

As we take a close look at the various tools of the social media trade, blogging is our first consideration. This is primarily because everyone, including you, has the power and ability to be a content publisher. If you can read and write, you're ready to begin. I further believe that your blog will be one of the most important aspects of your social media persona. Why? Because of all the content you ever post to Twitter and Facebook, you really own very little of it. Your voice is dependent upon the continued existence of the companies that sustain those tools. But a blog, assuming you back up its content regularly, is yours and no one else's. Therefore, your blog is a lot like the hub of who you are online—the business card that introduces other people to your various online profiles.

BLOGGING ISN'T ABOUT BLOGGING

When I became the editor of Pastors.com and Rick Warren's Ministry Toolbox newsletter, I knew from day one the goal wasn't "hits." And since we weren't selling products or ad space, the goal wasn't financial profit either. The goal has always been to expand our influence by creating and fostering community.

Blogs can be great writing platforms with all kinds of widgets, bells, and whistles, but the absolute best addition to any blog is people who return for the value of the content and the connections you provide. A community is made up of people who stay in tune with what you're saying, with you as the blogger, and even with each other in one way or another. Even before the advent of the Internet, a community was more than a mere geographical area within a set of prescribed boundaries. The word *community* has more to do with the relationships that exist among the people inside it and how they interact with one another.

A blog's community is enthusiastically tied to that blog's brand and content. Members discuss content with one another, discover new connections within the circle, and contribute to the value of the blog itself. A community actually begins to shape the nature and personality of a blog over time, and therefore a community can be grown but rarely controlled.

If your blog is going to thrive, then you need people to make contributions in the form of internal content (especially comments and ongoing discussion) but also to share your content with connections they have outside your community. One fact that Facebook understands well is that human relationships are far more important than directory listings and organic search results. Search results represent the infancy of the web, but having your resources shared is the future.

Without a community, your blog's success is always on its last leg. Its survival is dependent upon a returning, faithful audience that grows to trust you'll continue to contribute value to their lives even when you miss a beat here and there.

How do you start building community? The same way we've been discussing all along. Be social. Connect with people. Speak their language. Respond to their needs. Forge bridges of ongoing communication. Being social is far more important than joining social networks or using social tools. It's about cultivating real relationship—which is the real heart of the gospel already, isn't it?

How to Blog Awesome

Whatever platform you choose, the time to begin blogging was yesterday. We've already established the necessity of engaging the conversation around us, and since blogging is the best way to engage while owning your content, the question must be asked: How do you blog well?

Write blog posts for blog readers

As I've been learning the hard way at the very moment I write this, writing a book is a very different endeavor than writing a blog post. Books are obviously longer, but the structure of a book is also different. Blog posts must be written in a different style than a book, with a different structure and the design of the blog itself in mind. An effectively written blog post is written not only to engage the mind of the reader but also to appeal to the reader's eyes.

Blog posts don't have to be any particular length. Seth Godin (sethgodin.typepad.com) can tell a masterful story in about two sentences, while Brian Clark (copyblogger .com) may write a couple thousand words in a highly useful piece. What matters more is how the posts are written. Blog posts need to be broken up visually, not with the end of the page in mind, but rather the bottom of the screen, or "fold." Bullet points and engaging imagery are common on blogs, and most blog paragraphs are a couple of sentences compared to the four or five in a book.

Make sure the title pops

One of my pet peeves is a great blog post with a terrible title. I cannot stress enough the importance of a post title that pops. And when you're thinking what to title your post, remember that you're writing for two audiences: one human and one not so much.

The human audience is made up of your regular readers as well as the potential readers who will see nothing more than the post's title on Twitter or Facebook when you or someone shares it. That being said, it's pretty easy to imagine the difference in traction a post titled "The Jericho Road" would get from the same post titled "4 Ways to Meet More Strangers for the Gospel's Sake." Both titles could refer to a blog post written about Jesus's encounter with the woman at the well, and while the post itself might be chock full of awesomeness, only one of those titles will ever cause someone to click and learn more.

As you craft a post title for humans, make it interesting, address a problem that needs to be fixed, and clearly indicate the content of the post. Being vague or poetic really doesn't work well for attracting attention to a blog post on the web.

The nonhuman audience for whom you're choosing a title is made up of search engine spiders and crawlers, which are continually (hopefully!) indexing the content of your blog to serve up results to web searchers. All search engines worth their salt index the title of an article as the primary descriptor of the content of the article. In other words, a majority of the weight assigned to your post's relevance factor in search engine results will be dependent on the words you use in the title. With Google, in particular, only the first sixty-five characters of the title are indexed, and greater weight is given to words near the beginning of the title.

Why is this important? Because nobody is searching for "On the Jericho Road," but some people might indeed be searching "How can I meet more strangers?"

Engage the whole person

Great blog posts engage all three aspects of the personality of the reader: the intellect, the emotion, and the will. We engage and enlighten the intellect by making our readers think. This can mean creating tension in a post, presenting an argument, or introducing an idea. Engaging the emotions is a tougher task to accomplish. It really means helping someone feel something on the basis of the information we've presented.

I mentioned Mark Horvath earlier, the man behind InvisiblePeople.tv, and he's the ideal example of a blogger who has figured out how to dispense with heady information and boring statistics. Instead, Mark is a master storyteller. He puts real faces to a real problem most of us are mildly aware of and then challenges us to feel something rather than move on.

The third element of our personality is the will. It's the part of us that acts, moves, and makes decisions. In the blogging world this is referred to as issuing a "call to action," and the best calls to action are immediate, simple, and quickly executable. This may mean challenging people to leave a comment, share the post with their friends, make a donation, or make a purchase. If we've engaged both the intellect and the emotions effectively, calling the reader to action is much less of a hurdle to overcome.

Be predictably unpredictable

It's important for a blogger to show up regularly. My friend Ron Edmondson (RonEdmondson.com) blogs daily and has more than fifty thousand page views per month to show for it. Artie Davis (ArtieDavis.com), another friend, blogs only a few times per month, but his posts are hard-hitting and poignant. In either case, they're consistent enough that readers stay engaged.

While a blogger should predictably show up, it's also important not to lose one's spontaneity. One of the risks

117

of blogging on schedule is falling into a rut and becoming repetitious. If we fall prey to this habit, readers will lose interest and move on to fresher content.

Network with other bloggers

The world of bloggers is less competitive than you might think. In fact, smart bloggers learn to cooperate, cross-pollinate, and collaborate on ideas. Especially on social networks, most niche bloggers who share an over-lapping audience learn to respect one another and plug one another's material online. Just as car dealerships tend to group up in one part of town so they can catch the shoppers looking for the best deal, bloggers can share their audiences with each other quite successfully.

Don't forget about design

I will talk more in depth about web design issues in another chapter, but it's worth noting here that bloggers are not just authors of words but also artists who craft messages that include all the design elements surrounding their articles. The design and feel of a blog usually tells you something about the blog's author, in other words. Minimalism and white space usually say "my content matters more than anything else," while sidebars and spe-cial widgets say "I have more to offer beyond this article." Regardless of the style of the blog, bloggers should feature a design that acts as a frame, drawing the reader into the content well.

Integrate with social media

A blog that doesn't connect to Twitter and Facebook, allowing readers to suggest the blog's content to their friends, is missing out on an ever-enlarging potential audience. And a blogger who hides from his or her readers is missing out on the stickiness of a faithful readership. Every blog should feature, on every page, two things: links to the author's social profiles and buttons that allow readers to share a post with their friends with a single click.

TECHNICALLY SPEAKING

Starting a blog is easier than ever. There are plenty of ways to jump in, but some platforms offer a better experience than others. Thankfully most of the major platforms offer some form of exporting and importing between platforms, so choosing an inferior platform is not necessarily a fatal mistake. You can always switch with relative ease if you decide some other platform works better later on.

For now I want to suggest several possible ways to begin while zeroing in on what I feel is the most effective approach for getting started.

Tumblr

There is only one social networking tool outperforming Facebook in terms of usage among teenagers, and it's Tumblr (tumblr.com). Tumblr has three really great strengths: it's extremely simple to use, it's easy to use from a mobile device, and it's led by a team of developers who understand blogging is as much about images and

119

video as it is about written words. It's also free, but there are premium design themes available.

The reason Tumblr is taking off at such a rapid pace is because it is a tightly interconnected community. Tumblr users can "follow" each other's "tumblogs," so visiting Tumblr's homepage while signed into its service presents a stream of what other bloggers are posting. It also integrates well with various social networks, allowing users to easily share content across multiple platforms.

If all I wanted to do was start a simple blog in an easy way where I could post text, photos, and videos, I'd start with Tumblr.

Blogger

Blogger.com has been around for quite some time and has morphed a number of times in its existence. Many bloggers love it, but I've helped quite a few leaders figure out how to transition away from this platform and take their blogs elsewhere once they get the hang of blogging and start to take off with it.

Since Blogger is owned by Google, its future is only as certain as the future of any of Google's products. (Remember Wave? Orkut? Buzz?) With Google pouring much of its energy right now into the advancement of its social platform, Google Plus, Blogger has recently come to resemble Google Plus more closely, which may hint at its someday being absorbed or folded into the Google Plus platform in some way.

Blogger is very easy to use, but it has a few weaknesses worth nothing. Fewer and fewer talented designers are motivated to create templates for Blogger based on modern web design trends. Also, since it's built as a closed system, it has limitations when it comes to customization. Blogger is a possible option, but it's certainly not my favorite.

WordPress

Truth be told, I'm a WordPress nut—and have been since version 1.2 was released in 2004. WordPress is an open source platform, which means the code on which it is based is free to be modified, tweaked, and broken by anyone who wishes to try. This also means it is entirely developed by volunteers, and it has a robust global community of supporters to show for its approach. The core of its code is managed by Matt Mullenweg, its founder, and a company called Automattic, which has added many other applications to its portfolio, many of which extend the functionality of WordPress.

The first thing you need to know is that there are two separate versions of WordPress. The first is Wordpress .com, which is hosted by Automattic and is currently home to over sixty-two million blogs, most of which are hosted for free. Users pay money only if they desire premium features and themes. The second is a self-hosted version available from Wordpress.org. *Self-hosted* means that all the code that runs Wordpress.com is available for you to download and install on your own server or hosting space.

Here's the easiest way to understand the difference: you could visit Wordpress.com and be blogging within minutes, or, if you really want to unleash the publishing power of the WordPress platform, you can download and install the code from Wordpress.org on your own hosting space, which can be rented for a few dollars per month.

I love the functionality WordPress offers. For instance, in January 2012 we decided to move the entire Pastors.com website over to a self-hosted installation of WordPress. Within days we were able to implement a group of powerful new features, including multilingual translation, multi-author editorial management, and a version of the site just for mobile devices (a feature we've since outgrown). We control the code, the design, and the content on our own server, and the site's capabilities are extendable and expandable as the social web continues to evolve.

Clearly you have options when it comes to blogging, but hopefully this short tutorial has helped you understand the primary options available to you.

I opened the chapter with the bold assertion that everyone is a publisher. Obviously this is only true of those who choose to publish, but the option to do so is more readily available now than ever. If you're like plenty of pastors and leaders I know, you have a lot of wisdom to offer but an unwillingness or hesitancy to step out there. To you I would say: get rewired and start blogging!

Reflection and Discussion

1. If you're new to the world of blogging, what is your initial impression of what it's all about? How do you perceive someone who labels themselves a "blogger"?

2. How are you doing now with the concept and practice of blogging? Is it part of your strategy for growing your online influence?

3. Who are the bloggers you connect with and read? What can you do to learn more about the art and science of blogging?

4. If you're blogging now, what is one improvement you can make to your current strategy to take your message farther?

Chapter 11

I 'M A LOVER of Chick-fil-A. Most of my friends are too, and when Chick-fil-A comes up in conversation, a common story gets repeated. Beyond the tasty chicken, we talk about the hospitality, the extra-mile service, the fresh flowers on the tables, the efficiency of the staff, and the phrase "My pleasure." One time I visited the Chick-fil-A on North College Avenue in Fayetteville, Arkansas, on a rainy day, and not only did they give me more food than I paid for as a gift, but one of the employees opened an umbrella and walked me back to my car in the downpour! There are plenty of chicken restaurants in business, but none have the story of Chick-fil-A.

Every business and organization has its own story—good, bad, or ugly. To put it another way, they each have their own brand. You could most likely spot the logos of Nike, McDonald's, and Apple from a mile away, and you would immediately think of the company represented by each logo without any words or labels. The simple visual trigger of those logos causes us to associate the symbol with the identity.

But a brand is far more than a logo. As Phil Cooke has well defined it, "A brand is the story people tell about a person, product, or organization."[1] Branding is usually thought of as logo design, but it's so much more. A branding agency or freelance designer who offers services in branding is willing to help frame the story that gets told—and to tell it well.

THE "JESUS" BRAND

Jesus had, and still has, a brand—a story people tell about Him. Even in His lifetime this was true. In fact, Jesus referred to the concept of a brand once in a confrontation with the Pharisees:

> "To what can I compare the people of this generation?" Jesus asked. "How can I describe them? They are like children playing a game in the public square. They complain to their friends, 'We played wedding songs, and you didn't dance, so we played funeral songs, and you didn't weep.' For John the Baptist didn't spend his time eating bread or drinking wine, and you say, 'He's possessed by a demon.' The Son of Man, on the other hand, feasts and drinks, and you say, 'He's a glutton and a drunkard, and a friend of tax collectors and other sinners!' But wisdom is shown to be right by the lives of those who follow it."
> —LUKE 7:31–35

In this somewhat obscure story Jesus compares the Pharisees to a group of children who refuse to join in the games other children play in the public square. In those days kids didn't have Xboxes, so they used their imaginations and played fun games such as "wedding" and "funeral." In the culture of Jesus's time weddings and funerals were both town-wide, public ceremonies. Weddings took place over several days, and the bridal party would parade down the main street while the crowds cheered. In the same way, when a funeral occurred, the pallbearers would carry the bier or coffin through the middle of the town while the crowds wept and mourned.

Jesus then calls the Pharisees out on the way they cast John the Baptist as a wild man who must have been demon possessed and Jesus as one who partied so much, He must have been an alcoholic.

Interestingly Jesus reveals three different brands in the passage—three different stories people told about three different people or groups of people. First, He pointed out the brand of the Pharisees by essentially saying, "You guys are known as snobs. That's your brand. That's what people say about you." He indicated John the Baptist had a brand as well; when people told the story of John, they told the story of one who is melancholy and slightly aloof. And when people thought and talked about Jesus, the story was one of a jovial, happy, life-of-the-party guy.

Jesus's brand was like a wedding celebration.

THE YOU BRAND

You have a brand too. In fact, everyone does. And your personal brand as a Christian has a lot to do with what people think about the gospel when they think about you.

I was recently talking to a Christian leader about this concept, and he drew back with a sense of humility and said, "Wait, I'm not into self-promotion. I don't care about my personal brand. I just care about what people think of Jesus." I admired his attempt to keep his ego in check, but we don't have a choice about whether or not we have a brand. We all have a story, which is the essence of a brand. You have a brand, whether you're mindful of it or not.

The online world is a place where personal brands are amplified. Your name will travel along with what you write online, and it will travel farther than ever before. In the chapter on blogging, I wrote that a blog is like a hub of our online persona. Assuming that's true, your blog or website is the biggest factor in framing the story people will tell about you online. How it is designed, what you write or produce, and how you interact with others across social networks are all determining factors in how your personal brand is represented on the Internet.

If you're still completely uncomfortable with the idea of a personal brand or with the task of managing your image, just remember the challenge Paul gave to every believer to be an ambassador for Christ. That is, we are representatives of Jesus. As His followers, our brand relates closely to His, and our story helps frame His story. As you embrace the truth that you have a story and a brand, pray that God uses your story to highlight His.

THE CHURCH BRAND

Jesus is one of the world's best-known brands. More than half the world knows His story to one degree or another.

As we've just seen, you too have a brand whether you realize it or not, and your brand reflects on Jesus. The church also has a brand—a story people tell about it. In Western culture the brand of Jesus is maintaining pretty well, but the brand of the church is suffering. Since God desires to bring people to Jesus through the context of the church, this is a problem for our mission.

Artie Davis wrote in his book *Craveable* that when someone introduces themselves as a Christian, what goes through the mind of a person outside the kingdom is often something like this: "Before me stands a judgmental, mean, ignorant, and intolerant person. Why should I listen to anything they have to say?"[2] People perceive that the church has lost its way in the light of public scandals, personal rejection, and spiritual abuse. Our brand is hurting.

HOW SOCIAL MEDIA CAN SAVE OUR BRAND

It is not possible to concoct a story about the church that is better than what people actually experience in the real world, but it is possible to tell the *right* stories and to tell them well. Part of flooding the online space with God's glory and with the gospel of Jesus is making sure the gospel is given a great deal of attention next to all the other stories being told. This has been our mission since the beginning, and we now have more tools than ever for getting it done.

How can social media save our brand? It can't entirely.

129

If the story people associate with the church as God's people is to become a more positive one, it has to begin with our showing genuine love to one another and to the people living in proximity to us. Right now I sense another potential great awakening for the church that is less about creeds and more about deeds. Church leaders are pressing forward with their congregations to show the gospel and to be the hands and feet of Jesus to those around us. This is all good, and social media gives us the opportunity to share this story well.

Declare a cultural cease-fire

I'm not an advocate of compromising the truth as we believe and teach it. When it comes to social issues on which the Bible speaks, we must clearly and boldly side with the Bible. But how we go about standing for truth makes all the difference. In the online world Christians are thought of as intolerant, judgmental, and belligerent about issues of faith and morality. Without changing what we believe, we can certainly change what we emphasize. Right now most of the culture thinks of Christianity in terms of what Christians tend to be *against*. This is partly our fault to own. For a season of life in America Christians took up arms and attempted to bully our opponents into silence by rising to power over them. In particular, during the 1980s and 1990s we tended to believe that becoming a powerful majority in political life would allow us to legislate Christianity back into our culture. This didn't exactly look like the methodology of Jesus or the apostles, and in many ways it backfired.

Be for something

We have a chance to tell a different story—the story of what we are *for*.

For instance, my wife and I recently met with a staff member from a local pregnancy support center called Loving Choices (LovingChoices.org). She gave us some business cards to give to young ladies who find themselves unexpectedly pregnant. I noticed the slogan printed on the cards was "No labels. Pro Woman." The words *pro-life* and *pro-choice* incite a fight, but we're all pro-woman, or we should be. It's a different and perhaps better approach for the gospel's sake.

What if instead of being *against* gay people, we were *for* the dignity and respect of all people, regardless of sexual orientation? What if instead of being *against* liberals, we were *for* coming to a better understanding of how to help people in need in a way that makes sense? And what if instead of being *against* people with addictions, we were known for being *for* everyone's recovery?

Make a visible difference

I love the stories I'm hearing right now about the activity of the church in combating human trafficking and slavery, bringing healing to people with AIDS and HIV, working toward giving every orphan a home, and bringing food and clean drinking water to everyone in the world. These are the stories we must amplify.

I also love the current buzz I'm hearing about the radical grace of God. One of my favorite communities is People of the Second Chance (potsc.com). It's a loose-knit

131

group of creative people who work hard to tell the stories the world needs to hear. POTSC has a robust blog telling powerful stories in easily sharable forms. Their founding leaders speak around the world to raise a new "awareness" of grace. And they've just created a new church-wide campaign called *Freeway* that highlights their teaching about grace in a way that churches can grab onto it. According to their about page:

> We fight passionately against the forces of shame and judgment in our society but we do it with a smile. We boldly invite people into a lifestyle of grace both for themselves and others. By leveraging creativity, technology and a passionate online community, our organization is facilitating powerful life change.[3]

Yes! That's the mission! That's the power of creativity and social media to reframe the brand of the church, of what it is to be Christian, and of Jesus's impact in our current culture.

But if our brand is to be reframed, then our mind-set must be rewired for maximum engagement for the gospel's sake. That's what we need to discuss next.

Reflection and Discussion

1. How has our limited understanding of branding affected our ability to build a better brand for the church?

2. Why is it tough to think about Jesus having a brand? Do you think, according to Phil Cooke's definition of a *brand*, that Jesus indeed had a personal brand?

3. If a brand is the story people associate with a person, product, or organization, what would you say is the church's current brand in our culture? What is the story people tend to tell about the church as a whole? What about the brand of your church?

4. In addition to those mentioned in this chapter, what are some ideas for rewiring and reenergizing the church's brand?

Chapter 12

DESIGN MATTERS MORE THAN EVER

W HY DOES APPLE have a cult following? It isn't because of the low price point. It's about design. To Steve Jobs, Apple's late chief creative leader, design was far more than the outer veneer of a product. Design reflected the artistry that originated deep within the creator of a product, and that artistry merely showed itself in the product's outer veneer. To Jobs, design was less about aesthetics and more about function. He rarely criticized the products of his competitors, but when he did, he often pointed to the lack of uniqueness in them.

I'm convinced there are three kinds of people in the world: those who own and love Apple products, those who wish they did, and those who just don't know any better. My observation is offered tongue-in-cheek, and it's evident that I've bought into the Mac culture, where silver, white, and black are the best colors, and one button is pretty much always enough to do everything important.

I assert that design matters more than ever in terms of how we present messages, products, and ideas. We live in a culture saturated with rich design, and consumers are more sensitive to imperfections in design than ever before, whether they're aware of it or not. When you're surrounded by well-designed things, poorly designed things stand out.

Furthermore, I'm a big advocate of the idea that

everything churches do is communication. From the striping of the parking lot to the quality of the toilet paper in the bathroom, the little characteristics of your property's personality communicate a message about how much you wish to take care of your guests. The layout of your bulletin and the aesthetics of the slides on your screen communicate how clear you hope to be with your messaging. We tend to think of communication and marketing as one and the same to the exclusion of other areas of church life, but in the end everything we do communicates something about us.

The great thing about communication is that we control it, to some degree. We get to set the stage, create the environment, and establish a culture. We do this through design. I would define *design* as "the process of creating a product or experience that serves its user, solves a problem, and sends a clear message." Good design doesn't create a tension between form and function but includes them both as equal priorities.

WHAT WE DESIGN

Church leaders are more involved in the business of design than they usually realize. Remembering that design goes far beyond event flyers and weekend bulletins, we're involved in the design process continually.

We design processes for discipleship.

When I was a freshman in Bible college, I dreamed of two things: pastoring a church and marrying my fiancée. By the time I started my sophomore year, I had accomplished both. As a young full-time student and part-time pastor, my head whirled with ideas about how to structure a church. I filled legal pads with diagrams of how to organize people to accomplish the mission before us. I eventually learned that people don't always squeeze into diagrams we might create, but in the process I developed a love for the design of processes.

Every church needs to assess its philosophy of disciple making in light of the New Testament and then design a process for getting the task accomplished. Tens of thousands of churches have been influenced by the baseball diamond diagram that Rick Warren drew in his landmark book *The Purpose-Driven Church*. He took a simple visual concept—a baseball diamond—and used it to illustrate the process of moving people into membership (first base), maturity (second base), ministry (third base), and mission (home plate), with worship in the middle encompassing all the others.[1] This discipleship process designed long ago is still the framework for Saddleback's ministry and is taught to church leaders around the globe.

We design sermons.

As a pastor I never thought of sermon preparation as a design process until I started studying web design. As I began to understand the idea behind "information architecture" and "user interface design"—highly technical terms for web design geeks that basically boil down to how a website is structured for ease of functionality—I realized that while the larger part of sermon preparation is biblical exegesis and theological clarification, another part was designing the presentation of the sermon to grab attention, present information, and call people to action. A sermon without a well-designed structure may be theologically robust, but it won't transform lives until it is presented in a way that moves people from where they are to where God wants them to go.

We design worship services.

In plenty of churches, designing a worship service is a matter of choosing three songs and deciding when to take the offering. But churches that desire to reach the present culture think through many more elements in finer detail. A worship service is an experience in which people participate either actively or passively. It includes a variety of elements, and the number of creative elements keeps rising with the advent of certain technologies. Preaching and singing might be the primary portions of a worship service, but there is also presentation, video, and graphics; banners and staging; room aesthetics; responsive readings, drama, and testimonies; interaction via Twitter or text; and much more. While our goal is not merely to create an attractive performance, there is much to be said for the time and energy we put into preparing for the guests who will be present.

We design social media communication strategies.

My friend Jeff Gibson is a rare gem. He's a member at Saddleback Church and volunteers his time supporting Saddleback's social media presence. He is the quiet guy behind the scenes for several of the church's primary social media accounts, and it's a labor of love for him.

One of the reasons Jeff is so effective is because he's a spreadsheet nut who understands the need for a strategy with which to approach social media. Jeff thinks about who is listening to which networks at what times in various places in the world. He tracks responses and interacts personally. And he designs schedules for posting based on his data and his experience.

Jeff highlights the fact that social media shouldn't be a blind shot in the dark for churches. In a half-hour per day Jeff manages multiple social accounts for a megachurch, and his example makes it clear that with a little effort, we can think through our strategy as well. As you plot a strategy for your social footprint on the web, give some thought to who will post, who will (probably) listen, what you should say, and when you should say it.

We design marketing strategies.

Marketing gets a bad rap among church leaders. When we "market" the gospel, we get the feeling we're somehow becoming cheap salesmen for it, but marketing is very different from selling, and it's different from advertising as well. Advertising is offering a product, usually based on the marketing we've done for our brand, and selling is hopefully the end product of the process. But marketing is much broader.

Consider this definition of marketing:

> Marketing is the way companies interact with consumers to create relationships that are beneficial to both parties. Businesses use marketing to identify their audience before advertising to them.[2]

To paraphrase this for church leaders, marketing is the way churches interact with both members and nonbelievers to create relationships that are mutually beneficial. Churches use marketing to understand the lost and disconnected before sharing God's truth with them. Marketing involves understanding people and learning how to communicate effectively with them. When we design a marketing strategy in the church, we're determining how we will communicate with the world around us.

We design promotional strategies.

I live in suburbia—a neighborhood filling up with new houses in a community filling up with new people. Almost weekly I see in my mailbox a postcard from a church advertising an upcoming event or sermon series. This is what we typically think of when we think about our church's promotional strategies. But print advertising and printed promotional pieces are a shrinking portion of the church's promotional tactics. Of course, there is value in designing promotional materials with excellence, but one of the ways we need to be rewired is to return to thinking about our promotional strategy as *creating and engaging the conversation around our church and its message, which is the gospel.*

The question of how we will design promotional materials is pretty easy. A tougher question is, "How will we empower the people who *are* the church to engage people in relationships and to spread the word from person to person about the gospel and the value of a supportive community of faith?" We have better tools than ever for producing great graphics and nice materials, but at our core we should still give the priority of our thinking to the kind of evangelism that has happened in the church's history with or without the tools that technology affords us.

We design communication tools.

What we typically think of as promotional strategies, I would prefer to term as *communication tools.* Marketing is building a relationship between the church, its members, and its potential members. Promotion is spreading the word through those relationships. And doing well in both these areas means taking advantage of great tools for communication, including websites, mobile apps, bulletins, mailers, and invite cards. We also need graphics that represent our message in an artistic way for sermon series and events.

One of the aspects of communication design I love is that it empowers the 30 to 40 percent of church members whose gifting lies in creative arts. Historically the church has seemed to value teaching and organizational gifts over creative gifts, and this seems to be changing for the better. Don't be afraid to invite the creative members of your church to be involved in the process of designing your communication tools. It's a win for them, giving them a greater sense of contribution and belonging, and it's a win for the church, in that you'll have tools that effectively reach the people they're meant to reach.

Principles of Great Design

I notice good and bad design patterns wherever I go. I'm even a little weird about trying to identify the fonts I see on promotional pieces of all kinds (which is why I love the *What the Font?* mobile app!). I've been involved in designing for the web for more than a decade, both personally and professionally, and I've helped plenty of churches, companies, and bloggers design logos and websites. I've also been an enthusiastic part of the design community online, learning and soaking up all I can about the principles of good design.

Here are a few things I've learned along the way.

Good design seeks to understand the user.

Steve Jobs said of the PDA (personal digital assistant) that if you need a stylus, the designer has missed the point. He rejected hundreds of prototypes of Apple's products because of "feature creep," the problem of trying to squeeze too much functionality into a device outside the device's intended use. He tenaciously defended the user and protected user interface design.

Many churches struggle with this part of the design process, partly because we have trouble determining who the user really is. When churches are inward-focused, which is usually our default way of being, we think the end user is the church member who enjoys the rights and privileges of membership. When this is the case, we design websites and bulletins to be understood by people within our subculture, often ostracizing outsiders.

While it's important to give "insiders" a clear pathway from membership to maturity and mission, it is imperative that we see the lost and far from God as our primary audience and end user. In our design process we need to think about the first-time guest first, followed closely by those who need to grow, get involved, give, and go on mission. Understanding that hierarchy helps us to craft our communication to lead people to their next step in a way they can understand.

Thinking about the user means watching our language and communicating in the vernacular of the culture around us. It also means keeping our design uncluttered from distractions. One glance at the homepage of LifeChurch.tv, for instance, reveals that their design team understands what is really important to their intended user. Rather than trying to give equal weight to hundreds of ministries and programs, they give a few important links while immediately giving the user the sense that they've come home to a place where they're welcome.

Good design is both timeless and trendy.

Design trends change over time. In the last decade of web development we've moved from cluttered, tight, and information-heavy to simple and clean. We've moved from a dozen basic web-friendly fonts to a rapidly expanding field of typographical options. We've gone from animated .gif images to subtle patterns and letterpress effects. There is a happy medium to be found between being timeless in honoring our message while staying trendy enough to speak today's language, which includes more than just words.

Good design brings glory to the chief designer.

I believe God's glory is witnessed in all kinds of creativity, both inside and outside the church. Ultimately our commitment to excellence in design should be motivated by our desire to see and hear God's story told well, which is really the essence of why we design anything to begin with.

DESIGN MATTERS

When we think about our model for everything we do, it's impossible not to think about design. Christ, who created all things and holds all things together (Col. 1:15–20), had great purpose in the creation act and the way He has worked throughout history. He also was utterly intentional in the way He went about His purpose during His life on earth. Design matters to God—and so it ought to matter to us. It influences every decision we make, and it impacts the way our efforts are understood and received by our intended audience. It really is time to care about all we do and the way we design it. Are you in?

Reflection and Discussion

1. Try to assess your own eye for design. Do you think you can spot a well-designed piece of communication when you see one?

2. What are the values you hope to communicate with the branding and marketing of your church's or organization's promotional material?

3. List your own set of principles for quality aesthetic design. What do you consider essential and nonnegotiable?

4. What could you do to help improve your organization's ability to communicate your message through well-designed promotional content?

Chapter 13

THE FUTURE IS MOBILE

REMEMBER BAG PHONES? I never owned one because I wasn't rich enough, but they were quite revolutionary. They resembled the walkie-talkies used in World War II, but they had the tremendous advantage of allowing you to take your mobile phone with you in a leather zippered contraption containing enough electrical parts to construct a small aircraft. Opening the bag unleashed an entire mobile command center, and it made you look cool too.

We've come a rather long distance in a relatively short time when it comes to phones. My phone is a computer—an Apple iPhone, to be exact. It's seven millimeters thick, yet it contains an eight-megapixel camera that takes high definition video. It's loaded up with applications that allow me to track my finances, keep up with calendars and contacts, and even write a book. As an added bonus, it makes phone calls too. (We stopped using a landline phone several years ago because the only people who called us on it were telemarketers.)

Mobile devices are changing everything in our world. You might think that sounds a little overboard, and I might agree, had it not been for my recent trip to Haiti. The streets are lined with people struggling to find enough income to buy food for the day. The capital city is still in ruins from the earthquake that happened several years ago. And yet in a place where there is no television to speak of, people have mobile phones. I saw them peddled on the street corners like cotton candy.

The future is mobile, and the future is now. We've mentioned that the social media revolution itself is a cultural advancement that paves the way for the spreading of the gospel and that the Internet itself is a piece of technology enabling us to take the message of Jesus farther and faster than ever. In the same vein, the tectonic shift toward mobile technology is also contributing to our ability to move the gospel farther. Bibles no longer have to be smuggled into developed countries in suitcases. They can be downloaded to a phone or other handheld device.

PLEASE TURN YOUR CELL PHONES ON

I still chuckle when I attend a church or conference meeting and a slide displayed before the meeting starts asks people to turn their cell phones off. Right. Many have wised up and merely ask people to silence their phones, knowing full well no one ever turns a phone off. It also amazes me how many people fail to realize all it takes to silence a ringing phone is hitting the buttons on its side. This is almost universally true, yet so often in a quiet moment in a meeting, someone's phone will ring with the most obnoxious ringtone ever and the crowd waits in a state of annoyance as the phone's owner stands up and shuffles out of the room, fumbling with a ringing phone and sometimes answering it for all to hear half the conversation.

When we launched Grace Hills Church, we started asking people from day one to please turn their cell phones *on*. Why? Once again, people are talking, even during church. And we'd rather release our congregation to add to the culture's conversation in an immediate application of our pastoral challenge than fight against the inevitable behavior of a mobile culture. In fact, we've tried to make it easy for people to use their phones during our services.

One way we do this is by making our website mobile friendly. It adjusts to all screen sizes automatically, and we've created a mobile landing page (gracehillschurch .com/mobile) and forward visitors to that page when they access our site using our short URL (ghills.com). On this mobile-friendly page are several tools, such as an online version of our communication card, a message notes box that the guest can use to e-mail their message notes to their e-mail address, an easy-to-use online giving application, plus any weekly announcements. We also give away an ink pen that has a stylus on the opposite end so they can use paper or the web during services.

DESIGNING FOR THE MOBILE WEB

A couple of years ago I sat in a meeting with the communications directors from some of America's fastest-growing churches, and we talked about the trends worth watching. I was intrigued by the discussion about web development.

Two of the leaders talked about how they design for the mobile web, and one of them commented that when they design anything for the web, they start with mobile as their first consideration. That was a flip from the mentality I'd been working under, which was starting with the desktop computer in mind and tacking on a mobile-friendly version if the budget and system allowed for it. Maybe you can relate to this.

But mobile device Internet usage will soon overtake desktop Internet usage. Already half of local searches are performed on a mobile device. Americans spend 2.7 hours per day on their mobile devices. One-third of Facebook's users utilize the mobile version of Facebook, and half of Twitter's users do so as well.[1] We don't yet allow my ten-year-old daughter to have a Facebook account, but she does use her iPod for e-mail, and she's a nut about Pinterest—and her fifth-grade friends use their iPods even more than she uses hers!

Designing websites with mobile users first in mind is definitely a shift in our thinking about web development, but it's essential if we're going to be future compliant. Thankfully designing for the mobile web is not quite as complicated as it sounds. Whether you are in the designer's chair or you're in charge of the project without a clue how to write code, here are some factors to consider.

Keep it simple

When we use the words *simple* and *design* in the same sentence, most people get the impression we're going for boring or colorless, but this isn't the case at all. Simple design simply means keeping only the features and data that are necessary. Sales pitches in the old days included phrases such as "all the bells and whistles." But in web design, especially mobile design, less is more, and simple is better.

The reason simplicity matters so much in a mobile world is because of screen real estate. If I'm browsing your website on a cell phone, I don't necessarily want to scroll through dozens of menus and widgets before finally reaching the content I was searching for. Deliver the goods along with essential navigation and the features most important to the user's experience, and nothing more.

Keep it simpler

Yes. Keep it even simpler. Simplicity goes deeper than the page the user is reading. The system on which your website runs needs to use streamlined, up-to-date code that doesn't overload the processor in the user's device with dozens of query calls. Ultimately the goal is to get the necessary data to the user in a way that makes sense, solves a problem, and satisfies their searching.

Go responsive

A decade ago the web began to shift away from static HTML-coded websites built using tables to using CSS (cascading style sheets), which condense a lot of lines of code into a sheet that acts as a sort of template for a website. Pages could be produced more quickly and remain uniform in style by a simple tweak to the style sheet used

151

by all the pages that referenced it. Then the mainstream web moved in another new direction by moving from static data to database-driven websites, where the data displayed on a page was delivered up from a database via a query and displayed using the front-end HTML and CSS.

These two shifts were huge for the web and helped put the power of publishing in the hands of the average person, especially with the proliferation of open source platforms developed by communities of coders and made freely available for use by the general public.

Another shift has been occurring for the last couple years in the web design industry that has to do with the front end of websites (the part users see). It's called *responsive design*, which means the design of a site responds to the device on which it is being displayed. If you've ever browsed a website on your desktop and then pulled the same site up on your mobile device to find the exact same content presented in a way that fits the screen in your hand differently than the screen on your desktop computer, you've probably seen responsive design in action.

Here's why this matters to you. There was a short time when it seemed the web was moving in the direction of requiring separate sites be developed side by side for different devices. Mobile versions would be loaded as the user's web browser detected the device's screen size and served up the appropriate version of the site. This method is still widely used, but it usually presents a limited set of data to the user and creates a lot more work on the backend. It can also be a lot more expensive to design different versions of a website based on different devices people might use to access it.

Leaders in the design industry debate the question of whether mobile websites should be rendered via responsive design or by separate website versions determined server-side. While there are advantages to both, I see the trend quickly moving toward responsive design. As mobile device manufacturers continue to push the limits of speed and performance, page load time becomes less an issue than before.

The bottom line is: if you're thinking of starting a new design project or redesigning an existing site, go in the direction of responsive design and work with a designer who stays abreast of all the little changes in responsive design that seem to happen so regularly.

Adopt HTML5

HTML, the standard computer programming language behind most of the websites on the Internet, has moved through several major evolutions, all guided by a consortium of developers who determine when a new edition of the language is necessary. That consortium then attempts to influence browser makers such as Microsoft (Internet Explorer), Apple (Safari), Google (Chrome), and Mozilla (Firefox) to build into their newest browser versions the ability to render sites written with the newest editions of HTML.

HTML5 is the newest evolution of HTML and has been developed with the mobile web in mind. When Apple decided not to support Adobe's Flash format for rich media, mobile device users were unable to read or utilize much of the web's content developed in Flash, especially games and video. Maybe you've experienced this phenomenon for yourself when accessing a website on your phone, only to find that certain elements won't display.

HTML5 includes an attempt to render video and other interactive elements without the use of the third-party, proprietary Flash plug-in, which is owned and controlled by Adobe. If you embed a video on your website from Vimeo or YouTube, you're already using HTML5 via something called an iframe, but if you host rich media on your website natively, you need the ability to code the display of that media so modern browsers can interpret it—hence, the need to adopt HTML5. If all this sounds confusing and like it's written in a foreign language—which it is—don't worry. I'm just mentioning these terms so you're aware of them. Your next step will be to work with a web designer who already knows what these things are and will make sure your website functions with these tools.

When you need an app, make an app.

As opposed to responsive web design, which renders a website for use on a mobile device, apps operate in their own private ecosystem. Most of the nation's largest churches and nonprofit organizations have apps available for download from the various app marketplaces. In the world at large, apps typically function in a slightly different way than their native website counterparts. They offer interactive content not possible or practical inside a browser-based website. One of the biggest advantages is the app's ability to interact with the phone's operating system so that the app integrates with other apps, sends push notifications, etc.

In the world of the church, apps can practically duplicate all of the functionality of a website and coexist alongside the church's primary website and still be used widely. In fact, there's an advantage to releasing a native app for any church or organization, and that advantage revolves around the idea of community. I want to download my church's app because it's *my church*, and *we have an app*. Whether it offers any particularly special functionality or not, I want the app because I'm part of the community.

For individuals and leaders apps can be advantageous when the leader has a significant community gathering around media that works well within an app. The average blogger probably doesn't need a native app, but a pastor with a weekly radio program and a daily devotional might. Apps are great for media-rich content. People have taken slideshows about the gospel to the next level by releasing an interactive app in which one "flips through" a telling of the gospel story.

Be prepared to relearn it all again next year.

We live in times of exponential change, and this has never been more apparent than now, with the release of new versions of mobile devices and new operating systems in quick succession. With each new release comes a new wave of application environments, changes to base code, and greater complexity presented in simplified formats. So whatever you develop today, make it mobile and keep a loose grip on it. Be ready to change it all in a year if necessary. In other words, your website may already need to be rewired.

Reflection and Discussion

1. Think for a moment about the rapid move toward a more widespread use of the Internet on mobile devices. Reminisce for a second about flip phones, bag phones, or cans on a string. Why do you think things have changed so fast, and do you see the change slowing down at all?

2. In light of the rapid shift toward using the Internet on mobile devices, assess your church's or organization's readiness for this trend. How mobile ready are your current communications systems?

3. How are you using mobile devices in the life of your church? Can people take notes on their phones, get in touch quickly, tweet or post quotes from the sermon, ask questions?

4. What is a step your church or organization can consider implementing at this stage that would invite a more mobile world to engage with your message?

Chapter 14

T HE INTERNET HAS usually been considered an information portal in which you can find any kind of information you need, such as a globally accessible encyclopedia. At the end of your research session you simply disconnect. But the Internet today is much more like a cloud. Instead of connecting and disconnecting, we simply breathe it. It's a constant and steady part of our lives.

When I talk about using Twitter as an influence platform (or blogging, Facebook, and other tools, for that matter), I often say we need to "permeate the cloud that people are breathing." We need to show up where people are looking for relationships and answers. Twitter is a very good representative of that cloud. You can open Twitter at any moment and see the "timeline," which includes pretty much everything that's being said in that very second on Twitter. And millions of people are living there— reading, relating, and breathing.

YOU OUGHT TO CARE ABOUT TWITTER

Of all the social technologies available, Twitter is probably the easiest to write off as a toy rather than a tool. The reality is, however, that Twitter is far more useful than most people realize—especially for the purposes of spreading the gospel. Here's how.

Twitter forces us to concentrate our message.

If you take all the water out of fresh-squeezed orange juice, you wind up with concentrate, a far more potent solution. Twitter causes us to remove unnecessary words and reduce a message to its bare minimum. Obviously this can create the problem of lacking context and structure, but it also forces us to consider the reader. In fact, if we don't consider the reader, we can get in serious trouble.

So we have to ask such questions as:

- How will this be understood with no surrounding context?

- How will this reflect on my own values and beliefs?

- How could these words be misapplied by a simple misunderstanding?

- Is this valuable enough to be shared in the first place?

If you think about it, there's something pretty powerful about the exercise of condensing our thoughts and beliefs and messages down to their essential core. What will we communicate about the gospel in the span of 140 characters? What's the real gist? What matters most? Using Twitter helps us capitalize on the essence of God's message to a hurting world.

Twitter is a powerful collaboration tool.

When you can't find the answer to a question, ask it on Twitter, and you'll often wind up with a variety of opinions and perspectives. You can use Twitter to crowdsource the refining of ideas. Allow the crowd to help you brainstorm, refine, and pare down your message to its essential core. Just think how useful this could be when working on Sunday's sermon! It can also help gauge interest in certain events or activities your church is thinking of implementing. It's also an approach that lets people know we're as much about dialoguing about questions as we are about spitting out easy answers.

Twitter is a great real-time research tool.

I doubt you'll ever use Twitter to exegete a passage of the Bible in its original languages, but if you're attempting to gauge culture's understanding of a concept, measure a trend, or find a relevant application, Twitter can prove to be a powerful culture-search mechanism.

Twitter expands our circle of influence.

If you don't see Twitter's potential for connectivity, you haven't hung around long enough to test it out. You'll ultimately discover new listeners and readers as you build bridges with people you never would have known otherwise. I've discovered numerous great communicators and have allowed them to passively mentor me, all by hopping from one Twitter relationship to another. Our audience grows as we forge new relationships across social platforms.

What This Twitter Thing Is All About

There are plenty of philosophies and approaches to Twitter. Guy Kawasaki, one of the most influential leaders in the online world who also—fun fact—was one of the Apple employees originally tasked with the responsibility of marketing the Macintosh in 1984, believes you should expand your audience on Twitter as much as possible so your messages have the potential to travel farther faster. Robert Scoble, another technology evangelist who used to work for Microsoft, on the other hand, believes Twitter's more valuable for genuine relationship building and actual conversations. My peer Kyle Steven says, "Don't be a #TwitterSnob"—meaning that person who speaks but never listens, broadcasts but never tunes into the stories of others, and loves to be followed but never follows the lives of others.

Many people think of Twitter as an entertainment add-on to life's already cluttered nature, while others see it as an essential part of a successful business model. Me? I tend to think of Twitter in terms of the value it brings.

Twitter is about connections.

And by connections, I mean relationships, but the word *relationship* usually suggests something deeply personal. And Twitter, rather than being deeply personal, is usually a place where we make basic introductions. Out of these introductions, relationships are forged that often deepen to different degrees.

I would say I "know" Jacob Cass (@justcreative), a graphic designer from Australia. We've never met. We've never talked on the phone, but a church in Ohio recently e-mailed me asking for help with their communications and branding because Jacob recommended me to them as "the guy you need to talk to." That kind of recommendation requires trust, which is only formed as a relationship deepens. Jacob and I have never met, yet we've built that kind of trust and friendship through Twitter.

Also, because of the wave of celebrities and high-profile leaders who have made their way to the platform, Twitter allows us access to people with whom we might never have gained an audience otherwise. I once tweeted back and forth with Karl Rove about his years serving alongside President George W. Bush. Is that because he regards me as an expert in the field of politics? Actually, I'm fairly out of the loop in that arena, and Karl doesn't know me from Adam. But for just a second I had access to Karl, and he responded, all because he chooses to make himself available to normal people through Twitter.

Some relationships on Twitter turn into career opportunities. Case in point: my experience of coming to work with Saddleback Church, as I shared with you in the introduction. Others will never move beyond an occasional joke back and forth. Still others will be little more than a source of good links now and then. The point is, don't use Twitter without realizing its potential to introduce you to people who will influence you and whom you will influence.

Twitter is about content—short content.

Twitter gives you 140 characters with which to speak. Tweet too much, and people will tune you out, so you really have to be strategic about your messaging to get the word across. This is why content on other platforms (particularly blogs) matter so much to avid Twitter users. I can't explain quantum theory in 140 characters. I can't explain it at all, for that matter, but what I can do is tweet a link to an article about how fascinating quantum theory is.

When it comes to content, Twitter is an excellent content-curating tool. I have a list of people I follow because I know that they will consistently tweet links to helpful and inspiring content. They collectively make up one of the "newspapers" I read.

There's a negative but unavoidable aspect to this, though. Not everyone will like everything you tweet. But really, that's OK. The fact that Twitter is about content is highlighted by the value of what Twitter refers to as its "firehose" of information. Search engines and news platforms are sometimes privileged to have access to the entire stream of all tweets, which are like gold when deciding what kind of relevant search results to return to web users. In other words, Twitter will allow anyone to see a certain amount of data, but to large companies with a heavy media interest, they will allow those companies to pull an unlimited amount of real-time data. When I'm looking for a WordPress plug-in to accomplish a specific task, for instance, I often search Twitter for the most up-to-date results.

Twitter is about conversation.

This is what sets Twitter apart from search engines when it comes to content, and it's what makes connections happen. Twitter is definitely about conversation. The "@ reply" is a powerful tool.

Think of Twitter as a huge room full of chairs. They're all grouped in various little circles, and people are saying things. They're tweeting content, making statements, and asking questions. If Twitter really was that room full of chairs, what you would hear is chairs scooting around all over the place. People would be grouping up, then quickly moving to other conversations.

These conversations can have a powerful effect not only on individuals but also on culture itself. Consider Iran's "green revolution" in 2009 or Egypt's recent political crisis. Both events have unfolded differently than similar issues did in the past because of Twitter and other social media platforms. Suddenly oppression can't be carried out in a quiet corner but is talked about all over the globe.

IMPROVE YOUR TWITTER SKILLS

Just as we can expand our skills in any other mode of communication, it's possible to be a better tweeter if we learn lessons from those who have been around a while. Take these examples as your cue.

Follow people strategically

It's possible to follow way too many people on Twitter and create a polluted stream. The name of the game on Twitter is less about the quantity of people you follow and more about the relevance of what they tweet about. I try to follow all pastors, designers, and most authors who follow me, and I often scour the web for more potential sources of connection and learning. But I don't follow "social media experts," gurus, or multilevel marketers because I don't care to be marketed in a one-way conversation with people who often don't respect proper boundaries.

My tip to you: follow people who are talking about the subjects you care about and are willing to engage their audience in two-way conversations about those topics.

Engage people publicly

The point of Twitter is that it is a public conversation with your self-selected community of people. Obviously some personal conversations are best reserved for direct messages or e-mail, but when you're discussing your industry, area of leadership, or the gospel, there is tremendous value in doing so publicly. Recognizing others with a Twitter reply affirms their expertise and involvement or at least shows your interest in what they have to say.

Use a third-party application

This is not an essential tip, but it's a helpful one, especially if you manage multiple Twitter accounts—which can happen if you have a personal Twitter account as well as a more general church account on Twitter.

I'm an avid user of Hootsuite (hootsuite.com) on both my laptop and mobile devices. It enables me to create multiple tabs with multiple columns so I can monitor conversations I'm having through my own account, through our church's account, and through other accounts I manage. It also enables me to easily schedule tweets for the future.

Another of my favorite apps is Buffer (bufferapp.com), which allows me to post a message to multiple social networks and to space them out over the course of the day at times I've preselected. Buffer also offers a great web browser extension that lets me buffer articles I'm reading on the web to post at later times.

In short, third-party apps help you manage your social media accounts in a way that's less overwhelming than managing them all individually and in live time.

Find the balance between being personal and spiritual.

The late Dr. Adrian Rogers used to challenge believers to be "supernaturally natural." What he meant was that Christians should be distinctively Christian but also real, human, and personal. If your goal is to tweet the entire Bible in a month or constantly pump out in-your-face evangelistic messages, your missional effectiveness online will be severely hindered. It's vital to be personal, so feel free to post the pictures, jokes, and nonreligious observations you normally would share in real life. It's part of letting people into your life and establishing trust.

Respect the boundaries

Everyone is sensitive to spam and overt marketing pitches, the obvious goal of which are merely to milk relationships for money and attention. People are quite sensitive to sponsored tweets, and rightfully so, but they're even more sensitive to having their direct message inbox filled with messages from other Twitter users that are obviously impersonal pitches. "Thanks for following me—be sure to check out my blog/product/cause" doesn't work and ultimately pushes people away.

If you're new to Twitter, observe for a while before sending anything to anyone, publicly or privately. If you've been on Twitter for a while and you're still doing this, stop now.

The Value of Tiny Tweets

My friend Jeff Gibson, whom I mentioned in a previous chapter, is one of the smartest guys I know when it comes to the social web. As a volunteer he has been managing the Purpose Driven Connection Twitter account for quite some time. One day he relayed a story to me about receiving a reply to the account from a woman who simply asked prayer for her son who was in court at that moment. When Jeff replied, requesting more information and a promise to pray, she revealed she was sitting outside the courtroom in a country where spreading Christianity is illegal. Her son was on trial at that very moment for sharing his faith.

I had a similar experience in which I met a young pastor over Twitter who had just been ordained as a pastor and was beginning his ministry at a new church. I called him to offer congratulations. A couple weeks later

I was with two other Saddleback staff members on a trip through Texas, and we happened to run across the town where this young pastor lived. We were able to make contact and meet him at Denny's at 11:00 p.m., have prayer with him, and give him some resources for his ministry.

Is Twitter an effective evangelistic and discipleship tool? No matter how you argue either side of the issue, this much must be acknowledged: Twitter can open doors and pave the way. Twitter can be like a John the Baptist, the first messenger who prepared a pathway for the good news of Jesus Christ to take root. As Rick Warren likes to say, this technology is a gift from God for ministry. It's up to each of us to determine if and how we'll use it.

Reflection and Discussion

1. What was your initial impression of Twitter when you first observed or experimented with the platform? What do you think non-Twitter users probably don't understand about it?

2. How are you using Twitter personally? As an organization? What are the benefits you're experiencing?

3. If you were advising someone who was signing up for Twitter for the first time today, what would you share with them in the way of wisdom? How can a new user grow their influence?

4. What is something you learned or thought about while reading this chapter that could be applied in your sphere of influence to improve your current impact?

Chapter 15

MY WIFE AND I have rather different philosophies about household tools. When I need something such as a pressure washer or a reciprocating saw, I assume it's something I'll use again, and fairly often, even though I've never needed one before. So logically I need to buy my own. My wife, on the other hand, sees these items as somehow "nonessential" and assumes I may never need one again in my life. She therefore reasons that I should borrow one from a friend or neighbor. She's right, of course, and I have several power tools collecting dust to prove it. Besides, establishing a mutual tool-borrowing relationship with my neighbors is a way to live missionally, right?

This situation illustrates one of my greatest annoyances as a Christian leader, especially one with a keen interest in new developments in social media: I consider niche Christian social networks to be an abomination.

As editor at Pastors.com, I get a lot of news releases about new products in the Christian book and product world. I occasionally get an e-mail from someone letting me know I absolutely *must* cover their new Christian social network, which will be the biggest thing since Facebook—but for Christians.

Don't misunderstand. There are micro-networks

and online communities, such as FaithVillage.com, that I find very valuable as a supplement to what people are already doing online. My complaint is more with the mentality that we should come out from among the tools that already exist and do our own thing. It's a misapplication of the biblical idea of holiness and ultimately abandons a lost world to its own devices, removing all the salt and light from the platforms where people are conversing. Additionally it's wasteful of our resources to try to duplicate or replace existing networks that have already established themselves as primary hubs of discussion within our society.

In other words, it's OK for you to borrow Mark Zuckerberg's tools. Twitter, Facebook, Instagram, and a host of other online platforms have large and well-established communities that are growing by leaps and bounds. They are supported by multiplied millions of investment dollars and large development and support staffs. And they've weeded through the technical and cultural issues that matter to developers of social networks. So when it comes to getting the gospel to the furthest reaches of the World Wide Web, it stands to reason we would take advantage of these tools, especially since they are so freely offered for our use.

We're bypassing Myspace in our survey of the tools that matter to the cause of Christ and moving right into Facebook, which delivered quite a leg sweep to the former network when it opened its membership to the world outside college campuses. Let's talk about why Facebook matters so much and how to use it for good.

What You Share on Facebook Matters

Google is the Internet's primary search engine and serves as a sort of catalog of all of the Internet's hyperlinks. In a similar way, Facebook has etched its place in the online world as the ultimate guide to relational interconnectedness. Facebook is a collection of millions of overlapping relationships. While Google determines the relevance of a link by its content and who links to it, Facebook determines the relevance of content by calculating the greatest number of intersecting relationships that have affirmed its value with a like, a share, or a comment. This is known as the "Open Graph" on Facebook.

The best explanation of the open graph comes from Facebook's developers' site:

> The Open Graph lets apps tell stories on Facebook through a structured, strongly typed API.
>
> People use stories to share the things they're doing, the people they're doing them with and the places where they happen. Open Graph lets you integrate apps deeply into the Facebook experience, which increases engagement, distribution and growth.[1]

When I traveled to Moscow a few years ago to speak to a group of pastors, I was amazed at the connectedness we shared on the basis of our common place in the family of God as brothers and sisters. We didn't fully understand each other, and we probably would not have agreed on all

173

the finer points of our theology and social views, but we smiled and hugged and loved one another. When we finished our conference, the leaders of the Russian churches sang us a farewell song. That's personal connectedness!

I tend to think of the church and Facebook as being very similar. Just as in God's family we are delighted to discover our common spiritual rootedness in Christ, so on Facebook we enjoy the thrill of meeting a new friend of a friend or reconnecting with an old friend. When these connections are made, people talk, and what they talk about most is featured by Facebook for our other friends to see.

You may have been browsing Facebook under the assumption that you see everything your friends post or like, but this isn't the case. By default, Facebook shows you what it considers most relevant to you based on several factors, such as what you already like, what your friends have liked, and what is most likely to be spread farther. Facebook's selection may seem arbitrary, but it's really based on a highly tuned algorithm.

Why is the Open Graph so important to the spreading of the Christian message? It forces us to think not only about the content of our message but also how to communicate it in a way that is human, relevant, and engaging. Otherwise our message dies and rusts away in the scrap heap of irrelevance (at least according to Facebook's standards).

USE FACEBOOK TO ITS FULL EFFECT

Facebook is more than a tool for ministry. It's an entire toolbox. Let's talk about some proven strategies for utilizing Facebook as a relational tool for sharing Jesus and drawing people into a community of Christians.

Get personal with your profile

Here's a basic rule of Facebook that is continually ignored: profiles are for people; pages are for brands, organizations, and sometimes for public figures who have outgrown the five thousand friends limit of a personal profile. The real trick to using your personal profile to share the gospel is simple: be you. Talk about what you love—family, friends, favorite shows and restaurants, and your faith. As we've already discussed, you are interesting the way God made you, so realize that your personality, and therefore your Facebook profile, is interesting to people. Let the gospel flow naturally as part of who you are online, just as you do offline.

Use pages to promote brands and organizations and to build community

My recommendation for every church is to begin with a church Facebook page. As the page reaches critical mass, in terms of the number of likes, which will vary from one church to the next, then add pages for specific ministries or initiatives within your church's framework.

When we started planting Grace Hills, our Facebook page was our single biggest source of contacts. We purposely avoided spending any money on print advertising or direct mail and instead poured our resources into Facebook, believing its relational nature would be more effective at connecting us with people than the impersonal nature of print advertising—and we were right.

After a year and a half Grace Hills is one of the most liked church Facebook pages in northwest Arkansas. Along the way we've launched other pages for the different areas of our church, such as Grace Hills Kids, Grace Hills High (our student ministry), and We Love NWA (our big "serve the city" weekend each year). With any of our pages, the goal is to show up consistently and be helpful and encouraging. We ask questions, share quotes, post links to our events and message videos, and interact with other Facebook brand pages in our local area to establish goodwill.

Use Facebook advertising to reach a new audience

Facebook advertising is the only advertising we spend any money on at all. We've seen its effectiveness as a result of asking people how they heard about us when they visit, and quite a few have named Facebook as the source by which they heard about us.

Facebook advertising works well for several reasons. First, it's easy to target a specific audience. You can show an advertisement only to people who are married or single, who live within a certain radius of your location, and who fit within a certain age bracket. You can further target based on their interests, reaching only people whose friends are connected to your page but have not yet connected to it themselves. You can advertise your page, your website, or an event you will be hosting through Facebook's advertising channel.

If you're going to maximize your Facebook advertising investment, one of the keys will be testing. Run ads for only a short period of time, and then change them up. Change the graphics, the destination URL, and the descriptions. Try advertising your next sermon series or your next kids' event, and test the response. If you attract more likes, more traffic to your website, or more foot traffic of visitors coming on the weekend, you'll know you've figured out a smart approach.

Use Facebook events to make events more shareable

Whenever you create an event and post it on your church calendar or church website, also create a Facebook event for it. Then invite people you know will be coming. In turn, based on the Open Graph we discussed earlier, those who confirm their attendance will end up sharing and spreading the event to others who might be interested, as their confirmation of attendance will show up in their friends' news feeds.

Generate conversations as much as you broadcast news

Question marks are as powerful on Facebook as exclamation points. Leading up to a message series on finances, try asking your fans what financial habit they have found most helpful. Before a message series on the attributes and characteristics of God, ask people what they would ask God about Himself if they had the opportunity to do so.

Asking powerful questions has several advantages. It motivates people to engage with your page, it teaches you what is on the mind of the people you are reaching, and it shows you are as interested in listening as you are in talking—which is a big value of the social web, remember?

Use rich media

Facebook considers posts with images and videos to be more engaging than plain text or posts containing links, and they may be right. People love to share inspirational art on their Facebook walls, so supply their need by creating graphics featuring Bible verses and encouraging messages.

And don't be afraid to use a video camera—even the one in your cell phone—to shoot and upload brief personal updates to your page. It feels awkward the first few times, but people love the sense of a face-to-face communication. I once sat in my car and shot a brief video explaining what I would be teaching in the weekend message. My two-year-old son was in the video's background and yelled out randomly at just the right moment to illustrate what I was saying. I still get comments from people who were entertained by his well-timed antics.

Put a "Like" button on everything

If your blog or church website isn't capable of displaying a well-placed, full-featured Like button on every

Yes, You Can Borrow Mark Zuckerberg's Tools

page, redesign it today. The Like button is the quickest and most powerful way for someone, in a single click, to share your web-based content with all of their friends. And the more times a piece of content is liked, the further it spreads, and the higher it rises in Facebook's estimate of its relevance.

You can also put virtual Like buttons on almost everything you print, from T-shirts to billboards. Your page will be easy to find for people who live around your church, so a simple "Like us on Facebook" is sometimes enough to get someone to the right spot. You can also use QR codes and short URLs to get the word out by creating a kind of real-life hyperlink.

The bottom line is, you can't ignore Facebook for long, and you can't underestimate its impact on our culture. But you also can't assume it will remain the front-runner forever in terms of social media engagement. That's the nature of the social web—it's always changing. For now, though, yes, you can borrow Mark Zuckerberg's tools to share Jesus with your world.

Reflection and Discussion

1. Why does Facebook matter so much, especially now? Do you think Facebook outweighs other social platforms in terms of importance for the church? Why or why not?

2. What is your understanding of the social graph, and how do you see it affecting the lives of Christians and the impact of Christian organizations?

3. What are a few "best practices" for how the church should be utilizing Facebook as a communication and evangelism tool?

4. What is something you need to change or refocus on in your own use of Facebook as an influence platform?

Chapter 16

O NE OF THE more bizarre success stories of the Internet age has been the website I Can Has Cheezburger (icanhas.cheezburger.com). If you're not familiar with it, it's a blog offering what it calls "lolcats," daily pictures of animals (mostly cats) doing silly things with silly user-added captions. The website doesn't solve any problems in society or market any must-have products. It's just a collection of pictures of cats that will apparently make you laugh out loud. Amazingly I Can Has Cheezburger climbed the ranks of the blogosphere early and became one of the most profitable websites on the Internet with the advertising revenue it was able to gather. Most of us still don't get it, but we laugh anyway.

In the spring of 2005 YouTube went live. It didn't move out of beta until the end of the year, but it had already seen its first million-view video. Just a year later Google bought YouTube for $1.6 billion, believing it had potential. They were right. And in spite of being owned by a company that struggles with social products, YouTube is highly socially integrated with the rest of the web. But YouTube's real strength is its connection to the mainstream media. News organizations have realized the power of YouTube and have offered exclusive content on its platform, all the way up to a presidential debate.

(By the way, the I Can Has Cheezburger folks rely on YouTube to host their funny videos, so you can find cats that make you laugh out loud in either place, just in case you were searching.)

In October 2010 Kevin Systrom and Mike Krieger launched an app they'd been playing around with called Instagram. Two years later they sold it to Facebook for a billion dollars. Instagram had a million users in three months and is now installed on approximately 10 percent of all active iPhones.[1] There were already plenty of photography-related apps available, but Instagram found a way to design a very simple photography app that was also highly social.

I've taken note of a change in how my family uses photography, and maybe you can relate. We have owned cameras and camcorders before, with which we would try to catalog memories, create scrapbooks, and fill small storage boxes with pictures. On my computer I used to organize digitized photos into directories by year and occasion so they could be easily perused. But lately we don't organize our photos. We don't put them in any kind of chronological order. We don't even use stand-alone cameras for much of anything. Instead, we snap photos and take short video clips with our phones; post them to Facebook, Vine, and Instagram in the moment; and then we're pretty much done with them. This is why Facebook and other apps have moved toward a time-line model; they recognize people are posting memories in real-time in the context of a moment—a context that can now be preserved in the larger scheme of our lives because it's shown against the backdrop of all else that is happening.

It's Time to Get Visual

The bottom line for social media enthusiasts is that rich media (photos, videos, etc.) is big, both in terms of its content value and the social interaction that gathers around it. We didn't talk much about web content "going viral" before YouTube, but now that's a well-established term, as is the idea that rich media travels farther and faster.

The big implication for influencers is obvious: go visual. But how do we do that well? Well, let me give you a few ideas.

Be bold

For me and many others, video is tough. It's a little scary because it's so personal and so revealing—which is exactly what makes it so powerful. The people who are really successful with video are bold enough to put themselves out there regardless of their introverted personalities. Getting engaged in social media takes confidence, but video takes an extra dose of it. Some of the best advice I ever received about shooting videos was to overact—to be so animated that you're uncomfortable, realizing that to a video audience, you will only seem half as alive as you felt when shooting.

Be professional...or not

Sometimes video content needs to be produced in a studio or a setting that is highly professional, with professional editing and professional effects. Consider I Am Second's (iamsecond.com) use of the white chair and the black surroundings, for example. They've created a look and feel all their own, and the quality boosts the viewer's confidence in the end product.

Not all video has to be professionally produced, however. There is great value in personal, on-the-spot mobile video as well. Some of the most successful vloggers (video bloggers) in the market use their webcam or cell phone's camera to record. Often without any transitions or title screens, they upload raw video to the web, and it works. It's real. It's down-to-earth and personal. While I Am Second has been successful with studio-quality shooting, Children's Hospital of Los Angeles uses raw videos shot "through the eyes of hospitalized children" to raise awareness of what kids go through who suffer from disease.

Tell a story

The real beauty of rich media happens when it tells a story. For instance, our church set aside a weekend to serve the city. Since we're in northwest Arkansas, we called it We Love NWA weekend. We registered a domain (welovenwa.com) that pointed to a Facebook page set up just for the event. More than one hundred volunteers participated, serving nine local nonprofit organizations.

Leading up to the event, we used the domain and the Facebook page to recruit help. During and after the event we asked people to post photos from their mobile phones to Instagram, Twitter, and Facebook using the hashtag #welovenwa or #ghills. We then collected it all together and created a video story that was built by the crowd of people serving on the scene.

Media is more than raw data. It contains living stories that need to be told in fresh, vibrant ways that draw the observer into the storyline. This can be done with text alone, but it comes alive with photos and videos.

Spread it around

I've participated in various discussions about how to create viral content. Each time, I walk into the room knowing there are inherent difficulties with the task. Creating content is easy, but seeing it turn viral is another matter. Things go viral when they happen to be seen by just the right eyes at just the right time. There is usually no celebrity driving eyeballs to the content. It's spread from one average Internet user to another and appeals to something unidentifiable in the reader or viewer. Creating something that is popular is step one, but step two is completely uncontrollable. It's the step that takes place when something becomes more popular simply *because* it is popular.

Consider the Harlem Shake meme that broke out in the spring of 2013. Someone danced to a song in a funny way with a large group of people. It took off and appealed to people for whatever reason. It became popular, which made it more popular. People liked it more because other people liked it. Soon everyone was imitating it, and tens of thousands of Harlem Shake videos were popping up on YouTube.[2] No one could identify the primary drivers behind its success, and by the time it ran its course, the original version was lost somewhere within the meme itself.

Viral is usually accidental. Some brands have spent large budgets trying to manufacture something viral only to be disappointed. Furthermore, most of what goes viral isn't world-changing. Cute kittens and crazy dance routines don't really solve issues such as hunger and disease.

So let's scrap viral. Instead, let's go for a much older concept: influence. I would rather produce content that spreads at a moderate speed to a medium-sized crowd that acts on its message than something that's little more than a blip on the pop culture radar for a few days.

This is a visual, media-rich age in which we are sharing the story of the gospel. If you're not using images and video as a means of telling God's story, perhaps it's time for some rewiring.

Reflection and Discussion

1. Why are images and videos so powerful for telling stories? How have they become more accessible and easy to produce in recent years?

2. What holds us back from venturing into the rich media area of the social web? Why are we afraid to use video, in particular, to tell the story of the gospel?

3. Whom do you know who does rich media well on the social web? It could be a church, a company, or an individual. Who's telling stories visually that you should be learning from?

4. What do you need to start doing more of in the area of imagery? Shoot some videos? Create a podcast? Empower a team of volunteer photographers with access to an Instagram account?

Chapter 17

CULTIVATE YOUR NEXT-MINDEDNESS

WHAT'S NEXT? WHO knows?

Right now, thousands of start-up entrepreneurs are writing code and contacting angel investors in Silicon Valley in the hopes of creating the app that takes down Facebook or replaces Twitter. Some moderate success stories have arisen in the last couple of years, such as Vimeo (vimeo .com) and Pinterest (pinterest.com). They've found a unique way to subvert the power structures prevalent in the tech industry and carve out a niche for themselves.

As for hardware, we've witnessed the recent rise of the tablet and the slow merge of the tablet and the phone. (The iPhone 5 got larger while the iPad mini was in production.) Regardless of what new piece of hardware wows the world next, I think it's safe to assume we'll be swiping our fingers across screens for a long time to come. Samsung is a rapidly rising competitor to Apple's fan base, while HP, the one-time dominant PC producer, is struggling for life. The tech business is stressful for anyone whose fortune rides on a particular company's success, and consumers change their preferences with the weather. Keeping up is an elusive goal.

What we do know is that the church was once a community of early adopters, jumping on the bandwagon to use technologies such as radio and television for good effect, but it has since camped out in skepticism about the waves of technological advances in the present social age. This book wasn't written as a how-to manual for using social media, but rather as a challenge to the church as a whole, from the pulpit to the pew, to cultivate our next-mindedness.

Because of our biblical orthodoxy, we know God never changes and remains sovereign. Culture shifts quickly as it follows technology's advances, but Jesus still died on the cross for sinners and He is still coming again, in God's timing, to complete God's work of redemption. Heaven's completion is still in the works, and we who trust in Jesus are guaranteed that no matter what happens, we win in the end.

So drop your fear. Venture out. And be an example of the positivity that should dominate the outlook of those who believe Jesus lives today.

PROSPECTING FOR THE GOSPEL'S SAKE

Someone found gold in California once, and it changed the landscape of North America forever. In a decade a large part of the nation had gone west in hopes of striking it rich. A similar thing happened in Texas a century ago when someone struck oil, and more recently it happened in Alaska. Both states prospered so much from those discoveries that it wound up paying to be a citizen of either (through subsidies in Alaska and scholarships in Texas).

But for every success story there are dozens of stories of

washed-up lives who risked it all and found nothing but disappointment.

For believers in Jesus the story is different. Venturing into any new territory to share the gospel requires risk only in the fact that we don't know what will happen between this present moment and the grave. But beyond this life we have the absolute guarantee that God is gathering a family to Himself and that He has chosen the foolishness of preaching, or sharing the gospel, to make it happen. Prospecting, for us, is not a matter of taking a big chance or a blind risk. It's a matter of throwing our spiritual caution to the wind and striving for success in the confidence that God will accomplish His goals for the world and for eternity.

RAISING THE RIGHT QUESTIONS

I recently sat in a room at Saddleback Church full of some of the top thinkers in the world of church communications and social media. I hoped to contribute to the discussion, but even more I hoped to learn from it. So I sat with bated breath, waiting for grand revelations about the future.

We were asking three simple questions about the church in the age of social communications:

- How do we keep things simple?
- How do we keep things social?
- How do we make things viral?

I wrote down three big conclusions I drew from that night.

First, none of us know much. We know trends. We know tools. We have a handle on culture. We can articulate best practices. But things are moving so fast around us that none of us have it all nailed down.

Second, we are thinking, listening, and learning—all of which are more valuable than knowing.

And third, we live in times of unprecedented opportunities for world evangelism, in which borders (literal and figurative) are collapsing between nations, languages, and cultures. Because of technology more people are sharing their faith than ever before. There's plenty of room for debate about that, but I'm convinced evangelism is more doable than ever before due to the rapidly widespread access to technology as well as its affordability. From the proliferation of cellular towers to the ease with which we can manufacture MP3 playing devices, technology is beginning to level the global playing field and give people a quick and easy way to speak up for Jesus. And so my role as a pastor is to equip believers for ministry, which for me includes talking about how to use new tools, how to spread great content and ideas, and how to build real relationships in a virtual world.

At the conclusion of that meeting, I loved what Sherry Surratt, the CEO and president of MOPS International, said in summary: "I always consider a learning experience like this a success when we raise more questions than answers." As a pastor I struggle with the idea of raising unanswerable questions because I'm supposed to be an "answers" guy. What's the meaning of life? What did Paul mean when he said that? Will puppies and kittens be in heaven? I can answer those questions, or at least I can wing it and make it look like I have the answers. But the question of "What's next?" I don't know.

But together, let's keep thinking.

BIG QUESTIONS FOR THE CHURCH AT A CULTURAL CROSSROADS

Churches absolutely must change and adapt if they will remain relevant to the culture. I realize many Christian leaders don't like that terminology, so let me clarify that God's Word, the gospel, Jesus, and the church as Jesus intended it to be have always been, are now, and always will be relevant without our help. But we often hold on to extra-biblical traditions and ideas that severely limit our ability to communicate with a young generation, an influx of immigrants, and a culture being shaped by its technology and entertainment more than its religious and historical roots. In other words, if Satan's goal is to blind the minds of those who don't know Christ to the gospel, we often help him out by distributing the blinders of inauthenticity, racism, ethnocentrism, traditionalism, and political power struggles driven by fear and selfishness.

If God's desire to enlarge His family matters, if people who are lost forever without the gospel matter, and if the church of the future matters, we will embrace the pain of change for the win of seeing more people meet Jesus.

I don't have all the answers, but I think I have a few,

and they are rooted in my understanding of the gospel's effect on a community and my experience interacting with thousands of pastors and churches in the last few years. As I look at the landscape of stable or slightly declining churches that are fighting hard to stay afloat in the current of a rapidly changing culture, I see some common factors that must be addressed by church leaders.

Here are some tough questions I believe every church ought to honestly ask:

- Are we really all about Jesus? Is He the head? Does He have preeminence? Are we clear with people that it is to Jesus, and not to a consumer-oriented experience, that we are inviting them? Attraction is good. Jesus was attractive. But are we honest about whom we are inviting people to meet?

- Will we hold tightly to our historical, biblical theology? Will biblical inerrancy, which has survived a tough struggle in some circles, continue to thrive among evangelical leaders? Will we be faithful to the Word of Him who is the one and only way, truth, and life?

- Will we place our need to control, which is based on fear, on the altar as a sacrifice and begin to rely on the Holy Spirit? Will we trust His under-shepherds without the red

tape of boards, committees, and votes? Will
we listen to Hebrews 13:17?

- Will we embrace people from other cultures and backgrounds? Will we finally
put to death the idea of the "white church,"
"black church," "Hispanic church," etc.?
Can we value our cultural heritage without
the competitive idea that my culture is
better than your culture?

- Will we create a safe place for people to
deal with their hurts, habits, and hang-
ups in the light of the gospel? Can we
ever assure people we won't use their past
against them and handcuff them to their
shame?

- Can we grow up and get over our demand
for our own preferences to be met? Will we
be able to adapt our communication to the
language of humanity instead of church-
ese? Will we welcome newcomers with love
and wisdom, and will we listen and learn
from them rather than leaving the responsibility of adaptation to them?

- Will we make prayer and submission to
God the priority over polished productions
and performances?

- Will we take risks, spend money, change
names, reconstitute, relaunch, help the new

195

church plant down the street, and venture into new mission fields by faith rather than remaining safe and comfortable? Not all of these apply to everyone, of course, but will we take the necessary risks?

More than ever we need to keep our passion hot for Jesus, His truth, His church, new churches, new mission fields, unreached people, uninvolved believers, unforgiven sinners, the least, the last, and the lost. Pretty much everything else can be left behind.

So do some rewiring, dedicate your life to telling the Good News using every means possible, and go be the relational bridge that brings someone into a right relationship with Jesus—even if it does mean jumping on the social media train.

Reflection and Discussion

1. Why is it so hard to know what's next? And how much does it matter that the church be aware of new technologies?

2. Why are questions so valuable compared to thinking we have all the answers? In what ways might the church be writing its own death certificate as the culture develops around us?

3. Review the questions in this chapter posed to churches at a cultural crossroads. Which question jumps out at you as the one you really need to be answering?

4. How would you rate yourself in terms of your willingness to embrace and adapt to change for the gospel's sake? What can you do to improve and to be ready for whatever might be next?

I'M A NUT for a good link, which is a mark of a learner in this social age. And so, in what I hope is a useful appendix to this work, I'm revealing some of my favorite sources of knowledge and conversation about the social, digital age in which we live. The following is a collection of my favorites in the social media and marketing niche. To squeeze the most out of them, be sure to subscribe to them by e-mail (most of them provide an e-mail signup option on their home page) or via RSS feed.

SOCIAL MEDIA INDUSTRY INSIGHTS

- Mashable (mashable.com) is one of the leading voices in the social media arena, especially when it comes to news about developments in the industry, such as new apps and tools, changes to Facebook, Twitter, LinkedIn, and more.

- TechCrunch (techcrunch.com) keeps me updated on new start-ups and developments with tech-based businesses.

- MarketingProfs (marketingprofs.com) offers news and articles, but its real value is found in the short ten-minute videos that act as a how-tos on selected topics.

- Social Media Examiner (socialmediaexaminer .com) is a multi-author blog that brings together various perspectives of industry leaders in a very practical, how-to style blog.

- SEOmoz (seomoz.org) keeps me abreast of big changes in Google's search algorithm, which affects how we blog and design websites.

- Social Fresh (socialfresh.com/blog) posts short but great snippets about what's happening in the social media industry.

- *Fuel Your Blogging* (fuelyourblogging.com) is a wonderful online magazine about blogging, but I'm biased. (I used to serve as its editor.)

- *Fuel Your Creativity* (fuelyourcreativity.com) is another magazine in the Fuel brand group and covers the design industry with a broad stroke.

- Church Marketing Sucks (churchmarketingsucks.com) is operated by the Center for Church Communications and helps keep the church on track and away from bad marketing mojo.

- Media Salt (mediableep.com) provides relevant social media insights for church leaders and church creatives.

- Smashing Magazine (smashingmagazine .com) helps me understand design trends and provides free tools and challenging articles about creativity.

- WP Beginner (wpbeginner.com) is the best blog in the business about WordPress and covers updates to WordPress, apps, plug-ins, themes, and plenty of tutorials.

INDUSTRY BLOGGERS

- Justin Wise (justinwise.net) understands "social" as it relates to the church and offers solid application.

- Danny Brown (dannybrown.me) keeps it real. He has a great mind for marketing but also a humble spirit.

- Chris Brogan (chrisbrogan.com) is a consultant and author who understands social media like few other people on the planet.

- Seth Godin (sethgodin.typepad.com) offers a fresh perspective that usually challenges established ways of thinking about marketing. He's not always right, in my opinion, but he's always smart.

- Brian Clark (copyblogger.com) and his team are some of the smartest in the business of content marketing, which is the niche where I believe the church belongs.

- Tim Peters (timpeters.org) is a church communications specialist with plenty of fresh insights relevant to his niche.

- Phil Cooke (philcooke.com) comes from the creative video production world and understands branding and cultural movements like few others do.

- Kiesha Easley (weblogbetter.com) runs one of the best sites on the Internet for daily blogging advice.

- Michael Hyatt (michaelhyatt.com) talks about leadership, productivity, and publishing but spends a lot of time on issues related to blogging and social media as well.

- Kristi Hines (kikolani.com) collects and curates links and relevant articles about social media and blogging while writing tremendously useful content herself.

- Darren Rowse (problogger.net) has one of the best blogs about the business of blogging. He was in the game early and wrote about blogging before the blogging space exploded.

- Francisco Rosales (socialmouths.com) con-sistently publishes compelling blog posts about social media and marketing.

- D. J. Chuang (djchuang.com, socialmediachurch.net) gets culture shifts and offers a weekly podcast with leaders in the church and social media world.

As a final bonus, be sure to keep up with me at brandonacox.com, where I often write about social media, blogging, and marketing.

TOOLS TO MAKE YOU MORE EFFECTIVE AND PRODUCTIVE

T HIS IS AN age of tools and apps, and for this I am glad! It's easier than ever for creative people to take great ideas to market, find funding to make them happen, and distribute services via applications on mobile devices and the web. Here are a few of my current favorite tools for productivity and communication, plus a few I don't use personally but would if I could fit them into my workflow somehow.

- Springpad (springpad.com)—I use Springpad to brainstorm about projects and ideas in different areas of my life and work. Our staff even uses it as kind of a master bulletin board for all the projects and ideas we want to keep in front of us. There are mobile apps for every device, and the data syncs via the cloud.

- Evernote (evernote.com)—Evernote is probably the most popular notetaking and brain-organizing application among pastors (based on observation and conversation, not empirical data). It's not my favorite app, but most users I know swear it's the only way to organize your life, your research, and your planning. Ron Edmondson has written an excellent guide to Evernote called *Evernote for Pastors* (evernoteforpastors.com).

- Things (thingsapp.com), Omnifocus (omnigroup.com/products/omnifocus), and Wunderlist (wunderlist.com)—I find myself rotating regularly between these three different apps to manage projects and to-do lists. Wunderlist is the most simple to use and has the sweetest user interface, but Omnifocus and Things offer far more robust project management capabilities.

- CalenMob (via the App Store)—CalenMob is a mobile app I use to sync up with Google Calendar to manage all of my appointments and my travel schedule. It enables me to quickly view different calendars in a nice user interface.

- Notesy (notesy-app.com)—Notesy is a simple note-taking or plain-text writing application that I use on my iPad and iPhone. It's very scaled down and syncs with a folder in Dropbox.

- Documents To Go (dataviz.com/dtg_home .html)—Documents To Go allows me to create and edit documents in Word, Excel, and PowerPoint formats on a mobile device.

I wrote several portions of this book using Documents To Go, and I sometimes use it for compiling and displaying my teaching notes at church as well.

- IFTTT (ifttt.com)—If This Then That is one of the handiest online tools I've ever found. It's like a personal assistant for the social web. The concept behind it is simple. You create a little formula ("If I do this," which could be marking a tweet as a favorite or adding a new post to your blog, "then do that," such as adding a post to Facebook or bookmarking something to read later). There are dozens of apps and platforms that IFTTT works well with, and it's a huge time saver.

- Buffer (bufferapp.com)—Buffer is the primary means by which I post to Twitter, Facebook, and LinkedIn. I use the mobile app as well as the browser tool. It enables me to post quite a few updates at once but spaces them out for me so I don't overload my followers. Its benefits go much further as well.

- Hootsuite (hootsuite.com)—Hootsuite is a social media dashboard. Its browser app as well as its mobile apps stand alone right now in terms of a strong multi-column, multi-account social dashboard that not only offers the ability to post, read, and interact across several social networks, but also offers some built-in analytics for tracking one's effectiveness in terms of engagement.

- Tweetbot (tapbots.com/software/tweetbot) and Ecofon (echofon.com)—These two apps happen to be my personal favorites for simple Twitter-only management on my iPhone. Tweetbot is great for use on my Mac as well.

- Mindmeister (mindmeister.com)—Mindmeister is a mind-mapping tool. There are dozens of such tools available, but Mindmeister excels in terms of syncing with its mobile apps and allowing real-time collaboration and brainstorming for teams. If you're not familiar with mind mapping, it's essentially a tool that allows you to arrange thoughts spatially using bubbles and lines, but Mindmeister offers far more benefits as well.

- Gmail (gmail.com)—Gmail is the only e-mail solution for me. I use it to create a universal inbox for all of my various e-mail addresses and save e-mail so they're searchable over the long haul.

- Google Drive (drive.google.com)—Google Drive offers the ability to create and manage documents on the web. I don't use it as my primary publishing tool, but when I need to quickly share a document, it's often the best way to do so.

- Planning Center (planningcenteronline .com)—For church leaders, there is really no better solution for communicating with volunteer teams than Planning Center. It enables us to create schedules for volunteers in all of our areas of ministry and services and then notify those volunteers when they are scheduled to serve via text and e-mail. Our worship team uses it to collaborate about the message, the music, and other creative elements each week as well.

- Textmarks (textmarks.com)—Textmarks allows a church or organization to create a keyword. People can text the keyword to a five-digit number to receive text (SMS) alerts with news and information. It's a very inexpensive way to engage people, especially millennials, who tend to prefer texting over almost every other form of communication.

- Rapportive (rapportive.com)—Rapportive is a browser-based add-on for Gmail. It's

my "secret weapon" for discovering more
about the people I communicate with.
Whenever I read an e-mail or mouse over
an e-mail address, Rapportive shows me
any social profiles, recent tweets, and other
pertinent information about any social
media accounts associated with that e-mail
address. It allows me to follow, connect,
and friend people as well as interact with
their recent updates right from Gmail.

- Feedly (feedly.com)—Feedly is a news-
  reader that allows me to keep track of
  updated content on all of my favorite blogs
  and websites via RSS feeds. Since Google
  Reader shut down in July 2013, Feedly has
  become indispensible for me.

- Dropbox (dropbox.com)—Our church
  decided to spend money for a team
  account with Dropbox, which offers our
  church's staff a shared terabyte of cloud-
  based storage. We can each create our own
  folders, store files, and send links to folders
  to each other whenever we need to collaborate. Even for individual users with free
  accounts, it's one of the best solutions for
  syncing data over the web.

- MailChimp (mailchimp.com)—
  MailChimp is, by far, my favorite e-mail

newsletter marketing tool. Its features are
too many to name, but my favorite is that
it integrates so well with the social web,
which is rare among marketing tools.

- Pocket (getpocket.com)—Formerly known
  as ReadItLater, Pocket allows you to book-
  mark a story quickly for reading later in a
  simplified, mobile-friendly format.

- YouVersion (youversion.com)—I mention
  YouVersion here because it is, in itself, a
  social network that revolves around the
  Bible. It's also a tool that churches can
  integrate into their worship services in a
  dynamic way (via youversion.com/live). At
  present, it's been downloaded over one
  hundred million times and has helped to
  spread the Scriptures around the globe at
  an amazingly rapid rate.

Tools come and go constantly. My list will probably
look a little different by the time you read these words.
But tools and applications are ultimately responsible for
how we spread the message of the gospel online, so I rec-
ommend you make good use of those at your disposal.

NOTES

CHAPTER 2
THE DAY THE CONVERSATION DIED

1. W. A. Criswell, "The Beginning of Grace," Criswell Sermon Library, http://www.wacriswell .com/sermons/1946/the-beginning-of-grace/ (accessed September 30, 2013).

2. National Center for Injury Prevention and Control, Centers for Disease Control and Prevention, "10 Leading Causes of Death, United States" http://webappa.cdc.gov/cgi-bin/broker .exe (accessed September 30, 2013).

3. Socialflow.com, "KONY2012: See How Invisible Networks Helped a Campaign Capture the World's Attention," March 14, 2012, http:// tinyurl.com/7hrlvte (accessed September 30, 2013).

4. Charles Spurgeon, *Spurgeon at His Best*, comp., Tom Carter (Grand Rapids, MI: Baker Publishing Group, 1988), 67. Viewed online at Google Books.

Chapter 3
Relationships Can Save Everything

1. Goodreads.com, "Robert Frost Quotes," http://www
.goodreads.com/quotes/56899-good-fences-make
-good-neighbors (accessed September 30, 2013).
2. Anne Leland and Mari-Jana Oboroceanu, "American
War and Military Operations Casualties: Lists and
Statistics," February 26, 2010, http://www.fas.org/
sgp/crs/natsec/RL32492.pdf (accessed September 30,
2013).
3. ThinkExist.com, "Bill Hybels Quotes," http://
thinkexist.com/quotation/the-local-church-is-the
-hope-of-the-world-and-its/761846.html (accessed September 30, 2013).

Chapter 4
Now Is the Time to Get Rewired

1. Fredrick Levine, Christopher Locke, Doc Searls, and
David Weinberger, *The Cluetrain Manifesto* (New
York: Basic Books, 2000, 2001).

Chapter 5
Embracing Old Values in a New World

1. As quoted in Elmer Towns and Douglas Porter, *The
Ten Greatest Revivals Ever* (Ann Arbor, MI: Servant
Publications, 2000).

2. Fastcoexist.com, "How Social Media Has Changed How We Give," http://www.fastcoexist.com/1680994/ how-social-media-has-changed-how-we-give (accessed October 1, 2013).

CHAPTER 6
TO EVERYTHING, THERE IS A PURPOSE

1. Los Angeles Times, "United Nations Report: Internet Access Is a Human Right," June 3, 2011, http:// tinyurl.com/ppx5msf (accessed October 1, 2013).

CHAPTER 7
WILL THE REAL YOU PLEASE STAND UP?

1. Phillips Brooks, *Lectures on Preaching* (New York: Dutton, 1877), 5.

2. Lori Turner-Wilson, "6 Internet Marketing Myths Dispelled," *The Daily News,* September 18, 2013, http://www.memphisdailynews.com/news/2013/ sep/18/6-internet-marketing-myths-dispelled/ (accessed October 1, 2013).

3. As quoted in John Ortberg, Laurie Pederson, and Judson Poling, *Groups* (Grand Rapid, MI: Zondervan, 2009). Viewed online at Google Books.

CHAPTER 8
JUMP IN. JOIN THE CONVERSATION.

1. *The Week*, "Romney and Obama's Social-Media War: By the Numbers," October 22, 2012, http://theweek .com/article/index/235196/romney-and-obamas-social -media-war-by-the-numbers (accessed October 1, 2013).

2. Chrisg.com, "Building Credibility—The Value Shift," http://www.chrisg.com/building-credibility/ (accessed October 1, 2013).

CHAPTER 9
WATCH OUT FOR LAND MINES

1. Kevin Bonsor, "How Landmines Works," http:// science.howstuffworks.com/landmine.htm (accessed October 2, 2013).

2. Fight the New Drug, "How Is Porn Addictive?", http://www.fightthenewdrug.org/Get-The-Facts/ (accessed October 2, 2013).

3. Sydney Lupkin, "Can Facebook Ruin Your Marriage?", ABC News, May 24, 2012, http://abcnews .go.com/Technology/facebook-relationship-status/ story?id=16406245 (accessed October 2, 2013).

Chapter 10
You Are a Publisher, Like It or Not

1. Jenna Wortham, After 10 Years of Blogs, the Future's Brighter Than Ever," *Wired*, http://www.wired.com/entertainment/theweb/news/2007/12/blog_anniversary (accessed October 2, 2013).

Chapter 11
You Are a Brand, and Your Story Matters

1. Phil Cooke, *Branding Faith: Why Some Churches and Nonprofits Impact Culture and Others Don't* (Ventura, CA: Regal, 2008).
2. Artie Davis. *Craveable: The Irresistible Jesus in Me* (Lake Mary, FL: Passio, 2013), 1.
3. People of the Second Chance, "About," http://www.potsc.com/about (accessed October 2, 2013).

Chapter 12
Design Matters More Than Ever

1. Rick Warren, *The Purpose-Driven Church* (Grand Rapids, MI: Zondervan, 1995).
2. Mashable.com, "Marketing," http://mashable.com/category/marketing/ (accessed November 15, 2013).

Chapter 13
The Future Is Mobile

1. Danyl Bosomworth, "Mobile Marketing Statistics 2013," Smart Insights, June 20, 2013, http://www.smartinsights.com/mobile-marketing/mobile-marketing-analytics/mobile-marketing-statistics/ (accessed October 2, 2013).

Chapter 15
Yes, You Can Borrow Mark Zuckerberg's Tools

1. Facebook.com, "Overview: Telling Stories With Open Graph," http://developers.facebook.com/docs/opengraph/overview/ (accessed October 3, 2013).

Chapter 16
Let's Make Some Pretty Pictures

1. Kim-Mai Cutler, "From 0 to $1 Billion in Two Years: Instagram's Rose-Tinted Ride to Glory," Tech Crunch, April 9, 2012, http://techcrunch.com/2012/04/09/instagram-story-facebook-acquisition/ (accessed October 3, 2013).

2. Oddee.com, "10 Best 'Harlem Shake' Videos," March 18, 2013, http://www.oddee.com/item_98525.aspx) (accessed October 3, 2013).

FREE NEWSLETTERS
TO HELP EMPOWER YOUR LIFE

Why subscribe today?

- ❑ **DELIVERED DIRECTLY TO YOU.** All you have to do is open your inbox and read.

- ❑ **EXCLUSIVE CONTENT.** We cover the news overlooked by the mainstream press.

- ❑ **STAY CURRENT.** Find the latest court rulings, revivals, and cultural trends.

- ❑ **UPDATE OTHERS.** Easy to forward to friends and family with the click of your mouse.

CHOOSE THE E-NEWSLETTER THAT INTERESTS YOU MOST:

- Christian news
- Daily devotionals
- Spiritual empowerment
- And much, much more

SIGN UP AT: **http://freenewsletters.charismamag.com**

8178